MY STORY

MY STORY

THE LIFE OF DONALD BLAND

by DONALD BLAND
with Barbara Zimmerman

Library of Congress Control Number: 2024919684

ISBN: 979-8-218-51160-9

Interior Book Design by Tiffany Hiebert
Cover Design by Tiffany Hiebert and Kenley Ferguson

Cover Photograph:
Donald at Children's Home, Topeka, Kansas.

Published in the United States of America
2025 — First GTG Publishing Paperback Edition

GTG Publishing
1100 East 103rd Street South
Mulvane, Kansas 67110

*Dedicated to my Lord and Savior Jesus Christ
and to my loving and faithful wife,
Berniece,
who was the air beneath my wings.*

CONTENTS

FOREWORD

From the first time I heard my uncle Don Bland, my dad's foster brother, tell his story, I have been captivated by it. For years I've thought it needed to be put into writing so others may know of the work of God in his life — how He removed him, as a small child, from his biological family and placed him into ours. That was no mistake, for God's ways are not our ways. Though we don't always understand God's actions, His ways are much higher than ours (adapted from Isaiah 55:9).

Uncle Don has deep emotional scars from the events of his early life which in his 93 years, he has never been able to completely overcome. Though his natural parents were still alive, he was in every way an orphan when he was separated from both of his parents and his siblings. "…A child may be considered an orphan because of the death or disappearance of, abandonment or desertion by, or separation or loss from both parents."[1]

What may be viewed as a terrible mistake, God used for his good. In Uncle Don's heart, my grandfather, Cliff Bland, became his earthly father. Though Grandpa Bland died five years before I was born, I've "seen him" through Uncle Don's eyes.

Years later, following Uncle Don's repentance from sin and his faith in Jesus Christ, he influenced many people, including my brother and me, in coming to know his Heavenly Father as our Heavenly Father. I am eternally grateful to God for this man and for his witness to me! He is more than my uncle; he is also my brother in Christ. He has been my spiritual mentor, and I am thankful to know that we will spend eternity together in heaven.

I am also very grateful to my Lord Jesus Christ for the privilege He has given us to bring this book to completion. My husband, Darrell, has been a loving support each step of the way. He too loved Uncle Don very much and has patiently been my sounding board as I've bounced ideas off him to help Uncle Don's "voice" come to life in print. My daughter, Tammy, has been a wonderful encouragement as she helped me navigate my old, "dinosaur" laptop, gave me pep talks to finish the project when it seemed overwhelming, edited the work and answered many questions in how to accomplish this task. My niece, Jessica, has been an invaluable help in editing and tracking down dates and family history to verify or correct some of the time frames.

I want to thank Uncle Don's children, Donnie, Rob and Jody, for sharing their dad with me. I am so very grateful that they are my cousins! It is my prayer that this book will be a blessing to them.

It has been a true gift from God to have spent countless hours listening to Uncle Don share his memories in telling me story after story, which I have compiled into this book.

There may be some details which are not as clear as they might have been a few years ago, but we have tried to make this as accurate as possible. Some of the historical accounts here may be remembered differently by others, but these are Uncle Don's recollections.

In 1979, Uncle Don was able to obtain his records from the Kansas Children's Home and Service League. These documents shed much light on the struggles he faced in his youth and throughout his life. A portion of these records are typed in italics throughout the text. It is his desire and with his permission that I share this information with you.

I believe that you too will be amazed how God took an orphan, led him through great pain and suffering, and used his life to bring glory to our Lord Jesus Christ. This is his story.

Barbara (Bland) Zimmerman

INTRODUCTION
DONALD BLAND

It was on November 19, 1932, that I was helped off the train in Grainfield, Kansas. I was three years old, having been placed in an orphans' home almost ten weeks earlier. My siblings and I had been made wards of the court and were taken out of our home. I came from a large, poor family with an unaccountable, abusive, alcoholic father and a mother who didn't know how to cope with her world. The faceless man who delivered me to Grainfield and the two men who came to pick me up were unknown to me. The wind was blowing, and it was dark except for the dim light on the end of the depot. The man handed my small suitcase (which enclosed all that I owned and a little toy truck, the only memento of the past) to the man I was going to live with. This is the beginning of "My Story."

God has had His hand on my life and has always loved me. Even before I knew Him, He knew me and loved me. As I'm putting this together, I'm trying to the best of my ability to make it as accurate as I can. I want all the glory to go to God for His work in my life.

ONE

BORN INTO A CRUEL WORLD

Remembrances are few of my early life and of the family into which I was born at Dillon, Kansas, on October 26, 1929. The first thing I recall as a baby was seeing somebody, but I didn't know who it was. They kept looking me in the face and scaring me saying, "Boo, boo, boo!" I remember that so clearly. Neither my mother nor my father was in the scene.

During that period, there was constant turmoil in the family. I learned later in life that I had six siblings. I was next to the youngest in birth order.

The following information was granted to me (as an adult in 1979) from the Kansas Children's Home and Service League in Topeka, which I received by court order of the District Court of Dickenson County in Abilene.

Italicized sections are from records and direct quotes of case worker files from the Kansas Children's Home and Service League. The name changed to Kansas Children's Service League in 1948.

IN THE DISTRICT COURT OF DICKINSON COUNTY, KANSAS

In the Interest of DONALD SHUGART
a minor under the age of 18 years   Case No. 3388

ORDER

Now on this 1st day of May, 1979, the above captioned matter comes on before the Court. The above named minor, now an adult appears in person and requests the Court for an order allowing him to inspect the files contained in the above matter.

WHEREUPON, the Court being duly advised finds that Donald Earl Bland, who appears before the Court, is the same person as Donald Earl Shugart, the subject named in the above action.

WHEREUPON, the Court further finds that the records pertaining to Donald Shugart are in the possession, custody and control of the Kansas Children's Service League.

It is therefore, by the Court, ordered, adjudged and decreed that Donald Shugart, now Donald Earl Bland be allowed to inspect any and all records pertaining to Donald Shugart which are in the custody of the Kansas Children's Service League.

It is so ordered.
JUDGE OF THE DISTRICT COURT [1]

———————

Walter Shugart [biological father] born 2-6-93 at Hope,

Kansas,…had very little education. Since his marriage, has been unable to support his family. For a time, he worked on the railroad but was unable to keep that job. Does some trapping at the present time and some farm work for George Dillon, a distant relative…He is said to be quite a profane man and has always done a good deal of drinking. Seems to have no idea of responsibility and paid very little attention to his children while they were at home.

Cora Hunt Shugart [biological mother] *born March 12, 1892, at Carbondale, Kansas. Mrs. Shugart has suffered with* [poor health]*…for seventeen or eighteen years…Neighbors of the Shugarts feel that perhaps the abuse she has received from her husband is partly responsible for her condition…She, too, has always seemed unaware of her responsibility toward the children. She has never known how to cook and has had absolutely no system about her housekeeping. Mr. and Mrs. Shugart are said by neighbors to quarrel and fight constantly when they are together. He strikes her and she becomes almost insane and threatens to kill him, etc. It is said that many times she has chased the children from the house with the butcher knife. Since summer, Mrs. Shugart has been in Parsons, receiving treatment…Only a few weeks ago, they released her.*

The home, which is in Dillon, is a 4-room frame house, badly in need of repairs. Mr. Shugart says he owns this home, having inherited it from his parents. Inside, the place is very barely furnished and quite dirty, though not filthy. When Visitor [case worker] *called, Mrs. Shugart had all the window shades down, though it was in the middle of the day. There was a dirty, offensive odor about the place. The table in the kitchen was littered with dirty dishes and opened cans of food.*

Mrs. Shugart herself was in a dirty housedress and her hair was uncombed.

Marietta, [sic] *the oldest of the children, was born October 4, 1917, at Dillon, Kansas. She is said to be very attractive in appearance. The people of Dillon were up in arms about Marietta, since she ran the streets...and was apparently on the way to going bad. Her father used to run with the Mexicans who worked on the railroad and often took them home with him to spend the night and to drink home-brew. It seemed quite dangerous to leave a girl of Marietta's age...in the home. The Brown Home at Abilene became interested in the case and offered to take the two girls. Finally, Mr. and Mrs. Shugart consented and in January the girls were taken to the Brown Home. After they had been gone several days, the Shugarts wanted them back and tried to get them. They made all sorts of trouble but were finally told they would have the law on them if they did not quit troubling the girls.*

Lillian Dorothy, born in August 1924, is in the Brown Home with Marietta. These two girls are said to have improved marvelously. They seem to be very happy in the Brown Home and are doing fairly well in the school work. Seem to have no desire to return to their home.

Herbert, the baby, was taken next, early in the summer. He was about nine months old then and could not hold his head up. County authorities said he was the most pitiful specimen they had ever seen. He was placed in a boarding home in the country from Abilene and is coming out marvelously. He is now fat and well and is loved by the people who have him. They are thinking of keeping him definitely. [sic]

The four boys [Marion, Robert, Herschel, Donald] *who*

came to us were taken just shortly after the baby. They behaved just like little animals and needed a good deal of training in their boarding homes.[2]

———————

Final Order for Dependent and Neglected Child
State of Kansas, Dickinson County, ss.

IN THE JUVENILE COURT OF SAID COUNTY AND STATE.

In the Matter of Donald Shugart, a Dependent and Neglected Child,

Now, on this 14th day of September, 1932, came to be heard the petition and complaint of Thornton D. Scott, charging that Donald Shugard [sic] is a dependent and neglected child; there being present in court said child, Donald Shugart, and Cora and Walter Shugard, parents and Henry G. Engle, the Probation Officer, and Thornton D. Scott, county attorney.

The Court, after hearing all the evidence and being fully advised in the premises, finds that due and legal notice has been given to Henry G. Engle, Probation Officer, and also to Walter Shugart, parent, the person being in the care and possession of said child.

The Court further finds that the statements and allegations contained in the petition are true; that said child is a dependent and neglected child, has no proper parental care or guardianship and whose home, by reason of neglect, cruelty or depravity on the part of its [sic] *parents, of Donald Shugart, in whose care said child is kept, being an unfit place for said child.*

It is therefore by the Court considered, ordered and adjudged, that said child be given to the care of The Kansas Children's Home and Service League, 918 Kansas Avenue, Topeka, Kansas, with full power and authority…to exercise all the rights as guardian of the person of said child, with full authority to place said child in a family home with or without indenture, to be made a party to any proceedings for the legal adoption of said child, and in person or by attorney assent to such adoption.

Given under my hand, this 14th day of September, 1932.
(George Bisdroff) [sic]
Judge of Juvenile Court[3]

———————

I have no memory of my mother. Years later I found out that the one who took care of me was an older sister. I was told that one day she put me down on the floor, and I crawled over to a can of kerosene that was used for starting the fire in the cook stove. I somehow picked up the can and drank some of it. She said, "I saw it happen." She ran over, picked me up, held me upside down and pounded my back trying to get as much of the kerosene out of me as she could. She stuck her finger down my throat and said she did the best she knew how to do. Finally, she just put me down outside in the warm sun on the front step and prayed, "Lord, take care of him. I can't."

There were more family problems than anything good,

and I didn't know what was happening. I remember the day we were put in a vehicle and taken to the Orphans' Home in Topeka, then later we went to another orphanage that had a shiny wood floor.

I have a dim memory of being there. There were lots of kids there, and I was playing on the floor with a little toy truck. Some of those kids kept stealing it from me, and a person who didn't have a face would get it back for me and sit down on the floor and play with me. That part was a mystery to me because I didn't know who the person was. I slept in a high bed and couldn't get into it by myself. That same person helped me up into it.

Almost a month after my third birthday I was picked up by a gentleman from the Kansas Children's Home and Service League, put in a big limousine and taken to the train station. I was sitting in that coal-fired train and didn't know the faceless man who sat beside me. He took me to western Kansas.

––––––––––

[Notes from case worker] 9-17-1932 *Miss Forney brought the four Shugart children to Topeka, with final order, and word that the Commissioners had agreed to finance them.*

10-26-32 *Visitor* [case worker] *talked to* [a neighbor], *Dillon, Kansas, regarding the Shugart children. According to her, the people of Dillon have long ago quit helping the Shugarts. She says the children have run the streets from the time they have been old enough to walk. At first people felt sorry for the family and would give them clothing and food.*

[Neighbor] *herself took milk to them every day, but learned that the parents were drinking it all, and giving none to the children. Whenever she sent anything home with them, the parents used it instead of giving it to the children.* [Neighbor] *thinks it would be criminal to let the children return. They have been begging considerably in the past few years and she feels neither Mr. or Mrs. Shugart can or will take care of the children properly. Every day they* [children] *used to ransack the garbage can outside the grocery store for food.*

10-26-1932 *Visitor* [case worker] *talked to* [another neighbor] *of the Shugarts who says she has all the compassion in the world for Mrs. Shugart for she feels she is not responsible for her actions. Mrs. Shugart visits in the home quite a bit, coming there for sympathy and consolation. She feels that it has been a blessing for the children to have been taken from the home, but wonders how much can be done for them.*

According to [neighbor,] *Mr. Shugart is very lazy.* [Neighbor] *says the children have always been sadly neglected and that the Shugarts have been very selfish.*

The older children have always managed to sort of look out for themselves, but the little ones have suffered. For the past six months or so, Robert was always the one to see that the baby's milk was fixed, since Mrs. Shugart would never bother to take care of the baby's feeding.

11-12-1932 *Wrote Judge Bischoff of the…plans made. Told him we have a home for Donald.*

11-19-1932 *Donald was placed this date in a foster home with Mr. and Mrs. Amos G. Bland, Grainfield, Ks.*

11-30-1932 *Reported Donald's placement to Judge Bischoff.*[4]

TWO

A TIME OF NEW BEGINNINGS

It was a cold and windy November night when we stepped off the train in Grainfield. The man lifted me up and placed me on the gravel beside the track with my little suitcase. It was dark except for the dim light on the end of the depot. I recall that it was snowing. I was lonely and scared and did not understand what was happening. The big steam engine was so loud making a clanging sound "cloong, cloong, cloong." It scared me to death standing there by that big monster! The gentleman that brought me out from Topeka said, "You go with those two men over there." I didn't know who those men were. They started coming over, and I was terrified! He talked to them for a little bit, then he got back on the train and left. I had nightmares about that incident for many years afterward.

The two men turned out to be Amos Bland and his friend, Chet Newton, who ran the lumber yard in Grainfield. Amos told me, "Donnie, I'm going to be your dad." I rode with him, and he took me up to his house in the north part of Grainfield. He and his wife, Letia, had one daughter, Maxine, who was a year older than me. Amos had wanted a son, and Letia told him if he wanted one, he would have to adopt one. My presence there, I learned later, was for the convenience of not having to go through the process of childbirth, not having to suffer pain. I was there to have, not to hold, as there was no love shown in the family. Even though the home I had come from was horrible, being placed in a strange, new environment was very hard! I was so scared and not knowing anyone was devastating to me. I cried and had problems with wetting the bed and wondered where my faceless siblings were.

I was very upset at night, so Amos slept beside me in the bed to try to settle me down. Letia would stick her head around the corner of the hallway into the bedroom to see what the commotion was.

———————

[Notes from case worker] 1-6-1933 *Letter from Donald's foster mother saying he had just recovered from flu, followed by congestion of one lung. Had him in pneumonia jacket for four days, wanted health record when with his family. Miss Forney wrote the boys had frequent colds, one time she called when it was 20 degrees and found Donald and Herschel playing in the yard bare-footed and with little clothing on.*

2-8-1933 *Mrs. Mae Guy* [Walter Shugart's sister] *in office. Says she has been informed that Donald has been transferred to our office and she wants him at once…Was quite indignant when she learned the child was not here. Said she had papers with her from the court and she expected to have Donald. Also said that if he was placed for adoption, the foster parents would never adopt, she would see to that. According to Mrs. Guy, she went to Topeka two weeks ago and brought the three boys* [Marion, Robert, Herschel] *back, then had them paroled to cousins. That the League had no right to the custody of any of the boys, much less the authority to place them for adoption. Said the welfare worker who brought the boys to Topeka lost her job over this affair.*

2-13-33 *Mrs. Albert Dillon* [Walter Shugart's aunt] *called at the office and presented papers from Judge Nickles asking that Donald be returned. Promised to see an attorney and communicate with the Probate Judge.*

Consulted with Judge McClure concerning the case. It is his opinion that the purported decree relieving the Kansas Children's Home & Service League of the custody of Donald Shugart and ordering him returned to Mrs. Lorsen [sic] [Walter Shugart's cousin] *to be under the direct supervision of the Court was entirely outside the law and advised that we ask the Probate Judge to cancel the papers.*

2-15-33 *Called at the Probate Judge's office…Since the child is placed it is to his interest to keep his whereabouts unknown to the natural parents and for this reason no information has to be given even in Court.*

5-1-1933 *Joseph Hunt* [Cora Shugart's brother] *and another member of the family called at the office to ask where Donald was placed. He told how Mrs. Shugart, Donald's mother, was very much distressed because she did not know where he was. Said she cried much of the time because he had been taken away from her. He had considerable to say about the illegal procedure by which Donald and his brothers had been taken from their parents. We tried to explain that the League had nothing whatever to do with the removal of the children. Had simply accepted the children at the request of the court. That the League had been granted an absolute decree and with that decree had placed Donald in a foster home. Since the arrangement was satisfactory, was not in a position to give information concerning his whereabouts. This seemed to distress Mr. Hunt, and he left saying he would have recourse in the courts.*

...Mr. Hunt had gone first to the Governor's office in the State house and that he and the lady with him were sent over to the League office from there.[1]

Amos worked for the postal system carrying the mail from Grainfield ten miles south to Gove and then on further to Jerome. There used to be a grocery store at Jerome, and people could get their mail there. The job as mail carrier ended when the Democrats elected Roosevelt.

There was not much memory of living in Grainfield except playing with Maxine. I don't remember Christmas or special events. I do remember being shown off to both sides of the family and to friends as if I was a prized pet or whatever. It was scary with people looking at me like that. Even at that young age, I knew I was not a part of the Bland clan.

I was told later that the house where they lived was a mail order home — shipped into Grainfield in pieces. The pieces were all numbered and then put together. Letia's father, Claude Simmons, who was a carpenter, helped build it.

We lived in Grainfield until late 1934 when Amos and Letia sold the house there. I don't think they were able to make the payments on it. We moved ten miles south to a rented house east of Gove and owned by Dick Mendenhall. Amos worked very hard to support his family by delivering mail, hauling sand, selling horses and so forth.

We moved again to a rented farm by Shields, Kansas, south of the Smoky Hill River, in the spring of 1935. That summer was hot and dry. The drought began in all its fury, and the dirt storms were very numerous. Someone who has not experienced them could not envision the horror of them. They could come up at all times of the day or night. I recall one that came on a sun-filled day. There was no wind, very still, no noise, just as if the end of the world was coming.

There would be a dark black cloud on the horizon. It didn't make any difference from what direction it came, but it was usually from the southwest. It would get higher and blacker as if the dirt was boiling over the ground. When it got closer, the wind might come up or sometimes it would just settle in. Those were totally dark times.

Letia ripped up dish towels, wet them down in a dish-pan, and then Maxine and I would stand on stools to wedge those pieces of cloth down around the windows to keep the dirt from coming in. If we didn't do that, the dust inside the house would be so thick that we couldn't breathe.

That fall, at the age of five, I started going to a country school south of Gove. The school had only thirteen kids or so, and Ida Beesley was the teacher. She taught all the grades, and while she was teaching the older grades, we younger ones were listening and learning from them too.

If we were in school when the dirt storms came, Miss

Beesley would make us all huddle together around the stove in the one-room schoolhouse. She told us not to get scared, but it was going to get dark. It was a black blizzard. She would make a game of playing hide and seek. She had to light a lamp in there to be able to see.

After the storm blew over, Amos would come to get Maxine and me to take us home. It was scary, but Amos was there, and we were all in the house. That helped. We had quite a few of those dust storms. There were two years of them when I was in the first and second grades.

I didn't get to know Amos very well because Letia would get onto him every time I became the center point in his life. She would seldom let me be with him unless Maxine was there too.

One of the only times I remember that he and I were alone was right at the start of the dirty thirties when we went over to the railroad by Pendennis (a little town six and a half miles east of Shields) to get cotton cake* to feed his and Uncle Cliff's cattle. Amos had his two-wheeled trailer fastened behind his Model A and was pulling it to Pendennis to the elevator.

As we were going along, my hands were freezing because there were no heaters in those Model A's. When we got to the elevator, I went inside to the office where it was warm. Outside, they were loading one-hundred-pound sacks of cotton cake pellets onto the trailer. (As a kid, I used to suck on that cake.)

I stayed inside the elevator office because I was so cold. When Amos came in, he settled the bill for the feed. The

---

* Pellets of compressed cottonseed with the oil extracted.

guy in the office said to me, "Your hands are cold. You need a pair of these gloves." They cost a nickel and had an apple patch on the back of them. I don't know if the man gave them to me or if Amos had enough change to buy them, but I got the gloves. We went out and got back into the Model A.

On the way home, I told Amos I wanted a saddle horse for Christmas because he worked with horses, and sometimes he would take Maxine and me out to his brother Cliff's place west of Gove where most of the horses were kept. He had a colt that he was going to sell, and it was tame enough that he could put me up on it.

He said, "Well, you can ask for a saddle horse, and maybe Santy Claus will give you one, but you've got to remember that sometimes you don't get what you want." (I know why he said that because there wasn't much money for presents.)

Amos then told me the story about a little boy who asked for a pony, and when he got up on Christmas morning, he put his hand into his stocking and brought out a bunch of horse manure. The little boy said, "I thought I had a pony, but I guess he got away."

When we got home, Amos put the Model A away, then he took his single-shot rifle out and shot two ducks from a nearby pond. Letia would roast those for the Bland family Christmas dinner. In those days, we ate wild game. Amos did a lot of hunting in the winter with that gun. We ate a lot of duck, and they were greasy. When I got older, I didn't ever want to eat another duck.

All the while, I again kept on telling Amos I wanted a pony for Christmas. He said, "Be careful what you ask for because maybe Santy Claus doesn't have a pony." I said, "I know he does. We've got horses, and he's got a pony." He said, "Well, we'll just have to wait and see." He told me I couldn't keep asking for one all the time, but I was all geared for a pony.

That night was the usual Christmas Eve. I was told that I had to go to bed. Maxine and I were excited to see what gifts we would have for Christmas the next morning.

When we got up, I discovered Santa hadn't brought me a pony, but unbeknownst to me, Letia's dad, Claude Simmons, had made me a wooden rubber band gun. The rubber bands were cut from an inner tube. The gun had notches where we would put the rubber bands, and we shot one rubber band at a time. I also got another pair of gloves that Letia had bought for me.

Uncle Cliff Bland and his family came to have Christmas with Amos, Letia, Maxine and me. Everybody was there: Uncle Cliff, Aunt Ethel and their children, Clifford, Kenneth, Marie, Elinor and Wayne. By the time they got there, I could smell the ducks baking in the oven. They tasted better when we were able to eat them with company.

I was playing with my rubber band gun, and Uncle Cliff said, "Let me look at that gun. It might be just the right one. This looks like a straight shooter. Why don't you go over by the table there, and I'll shoot at you?" He said, "Bend over," so I did, and he shot me right in the backside. Everybody hooted and hollered all over about me getting shot in the behind. They laughed more when Amos had me repeat the story about the little boy whose pony got away.

Our two families greatly enjoyed the day! That was a

hallelujah time! I never forgot the story about the little boy and the pony, and for a few years afterward I was reminded, "I thought I had a pony, but I guess he got away." I would be asked, "Did you catch that horse that got away?"

THREE
THE BLANDS

A little bit of the Bland family history, as I was told it, is that Amos' parents, James S. Bland and his wife, Ida, settled in Gove, Kansas, because Ida didn't want to raise their sons in the "wet state" of Colorado. (Being opposed to alcohol, she preferred Kansas, a "dry state.") They had five sons: Jean, Forest, Cliff, Ross, Amos and one daughter, Vera. While living at Gove, James made his living by raising and selling horses and mules.

I remember Amos and Cliff out in Amos' yard tying a bunch of horses together bridle to tail and bridle to tail. They looked funny tied together that way. The men were taking the horses thirty-five miles south of Gove to the horse trader at Dighton. Away they went down the road on the east side of the cemetery. The man bought a lot of work horses for people to farm with, and the Blands would trade back and forth with him. If somebody wanted to buy a pair of mules, they'd find a pair for them.

Amos, Cliff and "Spec" (Forest) learned to Roman ride, which is riding two horses side by side while standing with one foot on the back of each horse. There was a bar that tied the horses together. It had a snap on each end that attached to the bridles of the horses so they could keep the horses running parallel to each other. The bar was used when training the horses, but I'm not sure whether or not the horses were held together with it during the races. Roman races were popular in that area sometime between World War I and the Dirty Thirties. Cliff and Amos were the brothers that would most often Roman ride, and I think they won their races almost every time they rode. I never saw them Roman ride because that was before my time, but I heard stories about it and saw pictures of them.

Before the road that came through Gove was changed, there was a grandstand on the north side of town. This was the site of the Gove County Fair Ground where rodeos and fairs were held. There were great days of celebration and excitement with all the different events to enjoy.

The Bland brothers, along with their wives, loved going to fairs together. They would go to the Trego County Fair in Wakeeney and stay in tents that, I think, were Army tents from World War I. Cliff and Jean would get up early in the morning. One of them would go to the hen house where the chickens were being shown, and he would get eggs for breakfast. The other one would go to the dairy barn and milk a cow, so everybody had a glass of milk. They'd come back from their rounds, eat their breakfast and just have a wonderful time together.

Spec, Cliff and Amos liked to hunt coyotes with their cars. They all had Model T's. They'd put the tops down, and whoever was driving would stand up in the seat and drive with his foot in the spokes of the steering wheel. They would shoot at the coyotes while resting the gun on the top of the Model T because it had a high windshield. The women were sitting in the back, and they were all screaming! I remember those days.

Because of the drought and the dust storms of the 1930's blowing away precious topsoil, farmers would plant alfalfa along the Smoky Hill River where there was more water. Hundreds of jackrabbits had overpopulated the area, and because they were eating the crops needed for livestock, they had to be controlled. Sometimes in the local newspaper, there would be advertisements about a jackrabbit drive which covered a large area. The farmers would bring in metal fences to clip to the posts at night. The next day, the rabbits would be chased into those pens where they would be trapped. The men would club them to destroy them. Guns were not used because of the fear of someone getting shot.

Another reason they needed to be eliminated was that they had boils and other diseases. I remember seeing those boils on the carcasses. The Health Department told people to stop eating them. It was best for the country that they were controlled. Cottontails never got those diseases. We could still eat them, and some people did.

After the rabbits were killed, they would be fed to the hogs. That was good hog feed. Boy, would the hogs grow fast, and they got vicious! When we'd throw a rabbit to them, they would fight over it. Some of the rabbit carcasses were taken by truckloads to mink farms in Michigan to be used as food for the minks.[1]

Uncle Cliff and Amos had a close relationship. They worked together with their horses, and later they decided to buy a carload of cattle in Kansas City. Uncle Cliff brought them out during the first part of 1935. They rented some pretty nice land down by Shields. It had a spring on it, but the grass dried up when the dirt storms were raging.

Amos was going to try to raise a crop of cane to feed the cattle. When he planted it, he didn't have the proper equipment. He used a chisel to make the rows, and then he covered the seed. He also made a makeshift planter by using empty gas cans. Holes were drilled every four inches, and then the cans were filled with cane seed. The seed would drop out through the holes. He pulled that implement with an old steel wheeled Fordson tractor that belonged to his father-in-law, Claude Simmons.

One day Letia drove their Model A over to the field where Amos was working. He was re-drilling some cane that had died because it wouldn't rain. It wouldn't rain at all! He lost his temper and started cussing. Letia came apart at the seams. She said, "Amos, Amos, the kids, the kids! Amos, the kids!!" Maxine and I were standing there listening to Amos cuss, and he knew how. Oh boy, did he!

Amos and Uncle Cliff didn't know what to do, so they took all the cattle east to Pendennis and loaded them up on the train and shipped them to Elk City, Kansas. There was not enough grass there either, so they had to load the cattle up again and ship them back to Kansas City to sell. Because there was no feed for the animals, poverty struck us again.

Amos and Uncle Cliff both lost their shirts.

Amos tried and tried and tried to make a living for his family. He was a hard worker! One time, he was trying to repair a tank which was used to supply water to the house. The windmill would keep the water level high enough in the tank so the water could run through a pipe to the house. When the tank leaked, the water level dropped, and we didn't have water. He got a torch and heated some tar to fix the leak. As he was getting out of the tank, he spilled the tar all over the back of his hand. It stuck to his skin, and when he started to peel it off, it took the hide with it. I remember all of that because I was standing right beside him. I tried to outrun him back to the house. He jumped a three or four wire fence slicker than a whistle. He went right up over the top of it and into the house. He didn't have anything in there to take the tar off. Letia put water on it, and that cooled it down, but it was stuck to him. I remember that very plainly.

FOUR
MORE MOVES

We lived there at the house near Shields for a little over a year then moved back again to the Dick Mendenhall place east of Gove. While living there, we got scarlet fever and were quarantined. Nobody could come in or go out because scarlet fever was a bad disease, but when it ran its course, we were turned loose. They took the plaque off the door that read, "No entrance! Scarlet fever!"

The dirt storms were still raging. One day it was as black as it could be, and the chickens went into the chicken house. Amos had put all the horses in the barn. It started raining, and then the sun came back out. The chickens came out of the chicken house, and the roosters were crowing. I said, "Do those chickens lay two eggs a day since they went to sleep, and now they're up again?"

We moved from the Mendenhall place to a house on the east side of Gove in 1937. Amos and Uncle Cliff found a job hauling sand for Highway 23 between Gove and Dighton. The sand was loaded into their wagons with shovels, then they would turn over the two-by-four floors in the bottom of the wagons, and the sand would run out onto the road.

I started second grade at Gove and continued up through the grades. It was a small town and a small school. When the children's worker came to the school to make her reports, it wasn't long before my classmates found out that I was an orphan. The name calling started (orphan, b_____, not belonging, no real parents). To combat the separateness and not feeling connected, I would get mad which led to fist fights, and I always lost. No love or support was given at home. I was told the problem was me and that I caused it.

As I was walking home after school one day, along came Amos with his wagon. He asked, "Where's your dinner pail?" I said, "Up at the schoolhouse." He told me, "Go get it." I went back, and a kid named Junior Priefert, who was four years older than me, was there. He made a smart remark to me, called me names and started slapping me around. He called me "Donkey Ears," so I called him "Monkey Face," and that didn't set well with him. When I got away, I ran around the schoolhouse. Amos asked again, "Well, where's your dinner pail?" I said, "It's still there." He left, and I thought he was going up to get it, but when he came back, he didn't have it. I asked him where it was. He said, "You go get it." I said, "I ain't goin' up there again!" He told me, "You go ahead." I went back, and Junior Priefert was standing under the canopy bawling like a baby. I think Amos kinda taught him a lesson. I grabbed my pail, got out of there and climbed back up in the wagon. We went home with the team, and Amos was done for the day.

Amos continued work hauling sand for the highway. It took many months to get that road sanded all the way from

Gove to Dighton with Amos and Cliffs' two wagons. The day they finished, Amos came home, and I was standing out in the yard. I told him, "Hey, you're home early." He said, "Yeah, I got fired." I said, "You didn't get fired. You're lying to me." He picked up a stick, spanked me and said, "Don't ever say that I'm a liar!" I learned the difference that day between teasing and lying.

[Report of visit to child] *11-10-1937 Donny* [sic] *is now eight years of age, tall slender, has brown hair, blue-gray eyes and seems to be normal in every way.*

HEALTH: He is in good health but has always been subject to colds. He seems to be outgrowing this and Mrs. Bland is hoping that he can overcome this tendency.

SCHOOL: Donny is in the third grade. He has worked hard every year and schoolwork is not very easy for him. Memory work seems to be rather difficult.

Financially, the Blands have had a rather difficult time. They have recently moved to Gove, trading their home in Grainfield, Kansas, in on a 160 acre farm which they now occupy. Most of the land is pasture and it will be necessary for them to rent land for farming. They came to the farm too late to put out any wheat and will have to struggle along for another year. They are now living in a ten room house, unpainted and very much in need of repair. This property was an estate, owned by the man's mother who occupied the property prior to the coming of the Blands.

When this family moved out, they practically cleared out the house, removed all the fixtures from the bathroom, took down the electric fixtures but were compelled to bring these back. When the family attempted to use the well, they found that it had been filled up and a heavy piece of iron wedged in. It will doubtlessly be necessary for them to drill a new well.

Mrs. Bland informed Visitor that she had some turkeys to market this fall and when she sold them she bought the children's winter clothes. In this way she was sure that they would have them.

DESCRIPTION OF HOME: They are only using the lower floor this winter. The home is very meagerly furnished, although the rooms were orderly and everything was neat and clean and in place.

Mrs. Bland stated they were milking cows on shares at the present time. In this way they had their milk and a small income. Mrs. Bland is optimistic and feels they can make a go of it if they are fortunate enough to have a few good crop years. Anyway, they felt that they had to make the effort.

RECOMMENDATION: Adoption was discussed with Mrs. Bland but she thought this was not the time to consider this and Visitor agreed with her. The family needs more security before entering into any definite arrangements in regard to adoption. In the meantime, Donny has a good home and will be given the care and supervision that he requires. He seems to enjoy the foster sister and Mrs. Bland reported that she did not feel they could be closer than if they were natural brother and sister.[1]

[Notes from case worker] *9-12-1938 Home call. Mrs. Bland…was interviewed. She reports that Donald is now in the 4th grade. He made his grade last year although he seemed* to lose interest for some reason about the middle of the school year.

Last year the children nicknamed Donald "Donkey Ears." This nickname cut deep, and Mrs. Bland thinks this may have been the reason for lack of interest in the school.

The family have always definitely planned to adopt Donald just as soon as they are financially able. Finances in the family have improved to a certain extent...Mrs. Bland stated...for the greater part of their living they were still dependent upon the returns of the dairy...

Mrs. Bland asked that a birth certificate be secured for Donald. She has had need of this several times but has explained to inquiring parties that she did not have one. This has served to date but she feels that the boy should have a birth certificate.

RECOMMENDATION: While the finances in the home are limited, we feel they have much to offer Donald. Question of adoption was discussed thoroughly with Mrs. Bland...We would recommend that final adoption papers be granted.

Case transferred to Hays Office April 1, 1940

5-20-1940 Donald Shugart, now Donny Bland. Placed with Amos Bland. This home is located at the northeast corner of Gove. It is a large two story house, a large barn and hen house located on the east side of the road. All of the buildings are in need of paint and look rather run down and in need of some repair. As one enters the house he is surprised to find the rooms in fairly good condition and the building to appear comparatively new.

A part of the rooms on the second floor were rented to high

school students. During the past winter Mrs. Bland has had two boarders. Mr. Bland has bought this place. He rents some land. They farm 200 acres. They have not been able to raise a crop for several years and have experienced many financial difficulties, partly because of Mr. Bland's health.

Donny and Maxine attend the Methodist Sunday School which is only three blocks from their home. They also are members of the Junior Christian Endeavor. Because of the chores Mr. and Mrs. Bland do not attend church regularly.[2]

The house we lived in was built in 1887. In 1921, Chester Cole dug a basement, poured a foundation and moved that house from the hill in the northwest part of Gove to a quarter section of ground on the east side of Gove. I'm not sure who owned it before it was moved, but at the time Amos and Leita bought the property, it was in the estate of Mrs. Cole. (I think it was lost in a foreclosure.) Her son, nicknamed "Shine" Cole, was mad about losing the house, so he cut all the wires loose from the ceiling and threw them away. There was no way to turn the lights on in one half of the house. There were even holes in the walls leading to the upstairs. I had to go up in the dark because there were supposed to be two light switches, one for down below and one for up above, but they were gone.

That's where I learned a little about wiring. I tried to figure out how to get some light in that part of the house by going down to the junkyard and getting old electric harnesses and wire that had been thrown away. I don't think I ever did figure it out.

One thing I did later was to connect a wire from the light socket hanging in the ceiling of my bedroom to the doorknob, then I asked Maxine to come up to my room. When she took hold of the doorknob, it shocked her so badly that she almost went over the banister. That got me into a lot of trouble! I learned not to do that again.

I liked to tinker with starters and generators and tried to get them to work. There was an empty bedroom next to mine on the second floor of the house. That's where I worked with those things.

(Many years later, my nephew, Bruce Wilson, owned the house and asked me if I'd come wire it. I said, "You betcha!")

We had milk cows, and we separated milk in the northeast room of the house. We also had an icehouse which is a hole in the ground with a roof built over the top of it. Amos and his neighbor, Pat Schaible, took their wagons and went down to the Hackberry Creek south of the Joe Losey place (where Uncle Cliff's daughter Elinor and her husband Lawrence later lived at the south edge of Gove). They cut the ice into blocks with a big, long saw and grabbed onto them with ice hooks, then loaded them onto the wagon. They brought that load of ice blocks back and unloaded them into the icehouse then packed straw around them for insulation. They filled up the icehouse, so we'd have ice in the summertime.

I remember getting down in there and digging through the straw to find the ice. After I found it, I'd chip a line on the side, then break it, bring it out in two pieces, and put it in the icebox. I had to open the top door of the icebox to put the ice in. The ice was also used to cool the milk down. They'd put containers of milk down in the icehouse to keep it from souring.

One of my hobbies as a kid was to make airplanes out of balsa wood. When I'd get a little money, I'd buy a plane kit, cut it out with a razor blade, glue it together, and then I'd have a little airplane. I loved making those planes, and I read stories about flying.

One cloudy day when Amos and I were outside, a plane circled over Gove, came around, landed in the pasture and taxied right up to the milk house. The pilot got out to ask if he could tie his plane down because there was a big thunderhead in the west. Amos, of course, said, "Yes." We got some ropes, and the guy drove some stakes into the ground and tied his plane to them. I was watching carefully. He asked, "Do you want to sit in it?" I said, "Yeah!" He put me up in that biplane, and I felt like I was "right there flying the plane." Afterwards, we went into the house. Letia had invited him in for supper, because in those days, there was no place in Gove to eat. He stayed overnight in the upstairs bedroom next to mine.

It rained quite a bit that night. The next morning, when the sun came out and it dried off, Amos and I went out with him to help take the ropes off the plane. As usual, I was all ears. He hand-cranked the prop to start the plane, ran around, got in and took off. I can still see that. I wanted so badly to fly in that plane with him.

Amos' friend, Joe Losey, bought his girls a Shetland pony. It never stayed home. It always came up to Amos and Letia's because they had work horses up there, and the pony liked to be with them. I was riding it one day while my friend, Dean Wilson, was there. The pony was stubborn, and I couldn't get it to go, so Dean hit it on the rump. It took off, and I was thrown to the ground. I landed on my left arm and broke it.

Amos was just coming home from mowing ditches for the county. He picked me up and took me to Doc Fagan's. The doctor set my arm, put a splint on it and bandaged it. Letia gave me fits because she said I caused it. She was angry that I couldn't help milk the cows, and she had to do it by herself since Amos was busy working for the county, so he couldn't help either.

That house was never painted on the outside when I lived there. There was also no sewer. The bathroom was that little square house out back. In the wintertime, we got pretty cold when we had to go outside to that little house.

One time, Letia's Aunt Luella came to visit for a while. Luella needed the outhouse and was in there when all of a sudden, I heard a great big crash. She was a rather heavy-set lady and had broken through the floor and couldn't get out.

I was outside at the time, and when I looked up, she had somehow managed to get the door open. She had her arms crossed in front of her and was hanging onto the threshold. Her feet were down in the pit.

Letia's dad had been building a granary at Letia's, so there was a lot of scrap lumber around. Letia told me to run and get some of that lumber to help get her out of there. I quickly nailed together a make-shift ladder. I took it to the privy, had her move back a little and stuck it down in front of her with an extra foot and a half or so on the top end of it. I told her to climb the ladder. She hadn't had much experience with that, but she finally did it. Letia was there and took her over to the back steps of the house. She told me to untie her shoes. I said, "No," and took off running to the granary. Letia untied Luella's shoes herself and got them off of her. (All this time, Luella was crying.) Letia didn't have running water, so she told me to go to the stock tank and get some. I brought it back a bucket at a time. It took a while, but they finally got her cleaned up. Claude Simmons came up and put a new floor in the outhouse soon after that. As time went on, it became a family joke how she had fallen through that floor. To her, it wasn't very funny, but rather an embarrassment!

———————

Claude Simmons would let me work with him to build things. One time, I took the circle cut-out seats from an outhouse, glued them together, added legs to it and made a little stool. I painted it and gave it to Amos. I made a little table too out of orange crates to give to Letia.

———————

7-28-1941 Mrs. Bland said that her father is very helpful with Donny, and Donny likes to take building materials to the home of his foster grandfather because Mrs. Bland's father is a carpenter and can assist Donny in making things. They have made such things as a little wagon with wheels that Donny found. While the children were visiting in Claflin, Donny was given the motor out of an old electric fan. He was interested in the oil wells around Claflin and when he returned home, he built a derrick and made a pump which he connected to this old motor. When he would attach it to the electricity, it would pump fast, and he had considerable enjoyment out of playing with it. Donny has unusual ability along mechanical lines.

Donny is doing better in school this year, perhaps because he likes his music teacher as well as his other teachers. He has gotten all good grades and made an A in one subject.[3]

FIVE

LIFE'S TURMOILS — SHEER TERROR!

About the time when I was nine years old, Uncle Cliff ran for sheriff and Amos started fighting cancer. It was in his jaw, his lips and his face. He fought that for about two years or so. He wasn't around much because of having to go to different doctors for treatment. He ended up at the Trueheart Clinic in Sterling, Kansas, which had a hospital and medical school.

"...Sterling for a time gained statewide recognition as a medical center through the Trueheart Clinic and its pioneer work in the treatment of skin cancer. Dr. P.P. Trueheart and his son, Marion, were the first in the Midwest to use X-ray and radium for this purpose..." [1]

5-28-1940 Mr. Bland had a lip cancer and also a lump which was cancerous under his jaw. For this he received... treatment...He has been to Savannah three times and has spent two weeks in October, December, and February. His jaw has not healed, and he experiences a great deal of a feeling of fa-

tigue. This sickness has cost considerable.

Mrs. Bland…said that the outlook for Mr. Bland's recovery was not good but they still had hopes that the treatments would eventually cure him. He has returned to Missouri two or three times since we last visited. The treatments have eaten the bone out of his jaw, entirely across the lower part of his face. He is sent home for 6 weeks rest between treatments. She said the wounds were very clean where they healed but they did not heal if there was any of the disease left. When Mr. Bland first returns home after he has been in the hospital for a while, he is very nervous. It is necessary for the children to be quiet and for them not to play the radio. In a short time, he is quite himself again. Mrs. Bland said she did not see how he could be as composed and cheerful as he is when she knows that he suffers so much…Mrs. Bland feels that Mr. Bland's illness affects Donny more than it does Maxine…

7-28-1941 Mr. Bland was in Savannah, Missouri, again having his face treated. Mr. Bland wrote his wife a letter in which he said that this treatment had been the most severe he had received and had required a great deal of courage. Mrs. Bland said she did not know what the outcome would be and seemed more discouraged than on previous visits.[2]

After years of treating the cancer, the doctors told Amos there was no hope for him to recover and that he was going to die. He got on the train to come home from his last treatment, and I remember Letia went up to Grainfield to get him. Maxine and I were eagerly waiting for him to be back, but when he got there, he was crying. That's the only time I'd ever seen him cry. Letia was also crying because of the news that he was terminal.

Of course, Maxine and I couldn't figure out what was going on. We were in the front room, and Letia said, "You kids get out of this room," and we did! I know she wasn't a very nice lady. I still try to understand that she was carrying one heck of a load, but she didn't have to take it out on Maxine and me like she did. I was completely baffled with no answers, and I wasn't supposed to ask questions.

It hurt me that Amos was struggling with cancer. I tried to show him that I cared, but he wouldn't let me. He was not very affectionate. It was during this time that I think I grew the most, but I was also the most lost.

I woke up in that house and heard all this commotion downstairs. I didn't know who was there or what was going on. I put on my clothes, went downstairs, and there was Aunt Ethel Bland, Letia and somebody else. (I can't remember who.) They were running back and forth from Amos' bedroom to the kitchen. They didn't see me, so I walked around the corner to see what was going on in the bedroom. Amos was sitting up in bed with a dishpan under his face, blood spurting into it. The cancer had eaten his face clear back to his ear. I could see into his mouth. Most of the time before, he had kept his jaw covered up.

He looked up, saw me, and growled, "Get the _____ out of here!" I know now that he was trying to protect me, but it scared me so bad that I ran outside to the barn. I stayed in the haymow the rest of the night till daylight. When I came down, I knew he had died. He had bled to death. It was terrible! The date was September 25, 1941.

The undertaker took Amos' body to Quinter, then they brought his coffin back to the house and set it in the living room on some kitchen chairs. Somebody sat with him all night like they used to do back then. Letia's sister Aunt Wilma Tustin and Aunt Ethel Bland were standing by the coffin looking at his body, and there was a little space between them. I thought if I could just get up there, I could see what he looked like, because I had seen him with no jaw, and that was scary! I'd never seen anybody that had died. The coffin was too high for me to see into. Aunt Wilma and Aunt Ethel thought I wanted to get closer, so at the same time, they put their arms around me and pulled me forward. My head went over the top of that coffin, and I looked at Amos in the face. His eyes were closed, and my face was right above his. I wiggled loose, scared as I could be, and ran out to the barn again! I stayed out there for a long time.

The Blands had an uncle from Crook, Colorado, named Charlie Owen. He was a brother of Amos' mother, Ida Bland. He was a big man, and he had hands that made about three of mine. He came over and put his arm around me, just about mashing me into the ground, and said, "Now, Don, you're gonna have to be the man in this family." I answered him, "No, I can't do that." He said, "Yeah, you got to."

I was eleven years old when Amos passed away, just one month and one day from turning twelve. I was completely empty and couldn't figure anything out in my life. My world was turned upside down…again!

Some people came to my aid and helped me after Amos

died. The ones that stood out in my mind were Uncle Cliff and Aunt Ethel Bland, Uncle Don and Aunt Wilma Tustin, Mr. and Mrs. Oran Daniels, Dick Mendenhall, Joe Losey and Fred and Arlene Crippen. I am thankful for them.

———————

12-1941 We received a Christmas card from Mrs. Bland in which she said that Mr. Bland had died. She asked us to visit when we were in the community.[3]

SIX

LIVING WITH LETIA

After the funeral was over, everybody went back home, and I continued to live with Letia and Maxine at the house on the east side of Gove. It seemed to me that I couldn't do anything right to please Letia. I never felt that she loved me. Although I may have, I don't remember ever calling her "Mom." She never felt like a mother to me. I tried to fit in, but trying to fit in with Letia was like trying to eat eggshells in a candy bar.

I don't remember her often making things that a boy would enjoy like a birthday cake or cookies or anything, but I do remember that one time either she or her mother made a pineapple upside down cake which is one of my favorite desserts. Our common meal was bread and milk. We'd break up the homemade bread and pour milk on it. Since we had lots of milk, that was a cheap, easy meal. She didn't cook a lot.

Letia had a dairy, and it seemed like she and I did all the milking. We'd take the milk to the separator room just off the dining room. My job was to take the skim milk out to the hogs. The cream was put in cream cans. We'd set it out on the side of the road, and somebody would come get it and take it to Grainfield. The empty cans would come back clean, and it was my job to bring them into the house. Our cream cans had little tags with our name on them, so we'd always get our own cans back again.

Letia was so tight that she didn't even want to use cream to make ice cream because she wanted to sell it. We would take some whole milk out to her sister and brother-in-law, Aunt Wilma and Uncle Don Tustin. Uncle Don had a hand-crank ice cream freezer, and we'd make ice cream out there. I would help crank it. That tasted so good!

Most of the time when we'd get together at Uncle Don and Aunt Wilma's, the men played croquet. They had an area fixed up real nice for that. I knew the girls from out there, Janet and Donna Tustin, who were Uncle Don and Aunt Wilma's daughters, and their cousin, Berniece Tustin. The girls would always run away to play, and Berniece's brother Richard and I were left behind. (Berniece and Richard were Uncle Don's brother, Harlan's kids.)

4-22-1942 Mrs. Bland helps with the milking. She has a hired man who is a son of the doctor at Gove. He worked for them during the summer of 1941. They found him good help and very dependable. During the storm in January, Mrs. Bland found it very difficult for her and her father to do the chores and deliver the milk. She hired the same man who was the son of the doctor, and he has been helping her since that time.

She said they have 26 cattle to take care of...She owns two brood sows, and they bought two pigs to feed the milk to after they had sold the fat hogs last fall. The income from the sale of the hogs helped very much with the expenses.[1]

At the age of twelve (only ten weeks after Amos' death), I was sitting in front of the radio listening to Gene Autry sing one of my favorite songs, "Back in the Saddle Again." Just then, the announcer came on the radio to say, *"We interrupt this program to bring you a special news bulletin. The Japanese have attacked Pearl Harbor, Hawaii, by air, President Roosevelt has just announced."*[2] The date was one I will never forget — December 7, 1941 — the beginning of World War II.

Soon after that time, the military raided and condemned the property of people living in a wide area in Gove County and surrounding counties. They used those counties for aerial training. The B-29's would circle away from the gunnery range and would fire bullets which were supposed to fall there.

(Afterward, when farmers got their fields back and were working them, they would find bullets and cartridges that hadn't even been fired. I remember that later Richard Tustin had a belt about six feet long which he'd found while farming. Another man, Allen Beesley, owned land ten miles south of Gove where there were a lot of cliffs. Some fifty caliber machine guns were found on his property. Farmers would check their discs because the clips would prevent those implements from working right. They'd knock the clips off and then go on farming.)

Life went on, and I had some good times with friends. There were about fourteen of us boys that roamed around Gove. We all had bicycles if I remember right. Clinton and Roger Faubion were two of those boys. Their mother, Lucine, lived in Oakley, and they were raised by their grandparents, Charles and Rose Swenson, in Gove. Some of the other boys that I remember were Lee Miller, Frank Morse, Donnie Crippen, Edwin Sanders, Loren Beougher and Dean Johnson.

We experimented with mischief like lots of boys our age. We would roll our own cigarettes and smoke them behind the courthouse. When we would get half sick, we'd head to Cooks' pond on the Hackberry Creek and skinny-dip till we got to feeling better. Then we'd get dressed and go home.

One time after swimming at that pond, we all started getting sick. Doc Fagan went down to investigate and found dead animals in the upper part of the pond. We didn't know they were there. He said nobody could swim there anymore. We were all confined to our homes till we got well.

When I was a little older, we would sometimes take our roller skates and get together downtown at night, choose up sides and play hide and seek skating on the sidewalks all over town. If we were quiet, we could hear the swish swish of the other team's skates and have an idea of where they were. We'd circle around on Main Street and then all of us would end up at the cement slab over the coal bin at the high school. That was great fun!

Another bit of entertainment for us in the summertime was when a man would come to town once in a while with a movie projector and a reel of film. People would get together to sit under the stars and watch a black and white movie that was shown on the north side of the old Brown's Store building. We'd take our popcorn or something else to eat and enjoy the evening.

There was a preacher who came to Gove, and he called the bunch of us boys "The Hooligan Gang." We would meet and have prayer or devotions at the church. He decided to take us to Scott Lake and stay overnight.

Fred Crippen drove the bus to take all of us down there. I had a comforter to sleep under that night and took some eggs and bread for breakfast the next morning. (I don't remember taking any meat.) When it came time to eat, Fred shared his food with me. I appreciated that. He cooked it for himself, his son Donnie and me. We played several games and had a lot of fun.

―――――――

Somebody from Kansas City used to send barrels full of good clothes to Gove to Anna Johnson, Aunt Ethel's mother. After everybody else chose something that would fit them, if there were any clothes left over, we would get some and wear them whether they fit us or not. One thing I got was a suit that was too big, and it had a vest with it. I wore that gray suit and vest to church at Gove.

———————

__-10-1941 Mrs. Bland...said that Don and Maxine joined the Methodist church last Easter. Donald belonged to the Hooligan Gang, a group of boys that was sponsored by the minister. About Easter, the minister asked if any of the boys would like to join the Church and Don volunteered to do so of his own accord. He attends Sunday School but does not care for church service.[3]

———————

Bertha Ulrich was our teacher when I was in the sixth or seventh grade. If the guys got their feet out in the aisle, she would tell them to stick them out there again, then she would step on them with her spiked high heel and put her weight on it. They learned to sit like they were supposed to, with their feet under their desks.

———————

Joe Losey raised lots of sheep. When a ewe had twins, most of the time she'd only let one suck, and the other one would die if not taken care of. These orphans were called "bummer lambs." Mr. Losey would bring them to town in a box in the back of his pickup, put them in a pen at Letia's and give them to me. I would take cow's milk and bottle-feed them when I got home from school. I'd give them a little grain too.

Dean Wilson and I were buddies. Well, he was supposed to take care of some of my bummer lambs while Maxine and I went to Claflin to stay about a week with some of Claude Simmons's family. He was to feed the lambs a coffee can full of grain every day, but instead, he set a five-gallon bucket of grain in there, and they all foundered and died.

Mr. Losey heard about the lambs, and when I came home from school one day, there was a sheep in the pen. It had a big "L" on its back. (That's the way Mr. Losey marked his sheep.) I told Letia, "That sheep belongs to Mr. Losey because it's got an 'L' on it." I rode my bicycle downtown to his filling station. I said to him, "There's one of your sheep up at my house. I don't know how it got there." He said, "Well, I haven't lost any sheep. It's not mine. I don't know who it belongs to, but it's not mine." So, I rode my bike home and told Letia that it wasn't his sheep. Later I found out that when he heard my lambs had died, he picked out one of his best sheep and put it in the pen while I was at school. He was a good man, and I'm thankful for him.

I raised more orphan lambs and sold them at the sale barn in Oakley, thirty miles northwest of Gove. Letia didn't like it that I kept the money from them because she thought I should be the bread winner and give the money to her. Instead, I bought a bicycle. When Letia saw the bike, she was upset and said, "The government is going to come get that because it's made out of aluminum, and you're going to lose it." That scared me to death! She was a bear cat! She did a lot of lying to me. The more she lied, the more I didn't pay any attention to her, and the more I didn't pay attention to her, the madder she got!

When it came time for me to get my driver's license [permit], I needed to have an adult go with me to the hardware store in Gove so they could sign for me. The cost for the license was fifty cents. Another requirement was that they wanted to see a copy of my birth certificate. I did not have mine, so when the representative from the Kansas Children's Home and Service League came out to Gove to report on how I was getting along, I asked her if she could get my birth certificate for me.

4-22-1942 Donny was interested in talking to us about his birth certificate. Because of the recent discussion of birth certificates, Donny has been interested to know if he could succeed in getting his since he is an adopted [foster] *child. We promised to take the matter up at the Wichita office and see if a birth certificate could not be gotten for him.*[4]

When I received it, I was shocked when I read the name Donald Shugart, and that I was born in a place called Dillon, Kansas. I did not know that name! When I came to Gove as a child, I was called Donnie Bland. That's the only name I knew, and I had no idea where Dillon, Kansas, was.

This added to my longing to find out who I was. I never felt that I belonged to anyone since Amos died. I needed to find "home." I thought about running away and going down to Dighton because the railroad went through there. I said to myself, "I'll walk down there and find out if there's anybody out there who knows who I am." Even though it was thirty-five miles to Dighton, I knew I had to go to find answers. Letia didn't travel in that direction. She always went north, and I didn't think she would find me if I headed south. I never did do it, but I was ready to.

There was more trouble brewing at home. I remember the time when I was feeding cattle, and I guess Letia didn't think I did it right. One cold winter day, I went out to feed them. It was snowing. I went over to our neighbor, Andrew Anderson's place, got an oil can full of white gas and took it back home. That 1929 John Deere D tractor had a cup where you'd pour some gas in. I did that, then got water out of the stock tank, put the drain plug in the tractor and filled the radiator. I knew it wouldn't freeze as long as it was running. (Since we didn't have antifreeze, we always had to drain the water out of the tractor when we were finished using it.)

I was so small that I could hardly get up on the tractor. I had to put one foot on the front of the tractor and the other foot on the lug. I drove the tractor around to the corral to hook up to a wagon that Amos had made for hauling cane. I pulled it out on the highway and went north out of Gove. Nobody said a word to me about not doing that. When I got up there to where the feed was, I loaded all the bundles I could. I couldn't use a pitchfork, so I had to pick them up by hand and throw them up onto the wagon. Finally, I got it level with feed. In the process of doing that, I got sopping wet. My teeth were chattering!

I drove the tractor back through the pasture and up to the corral at Letia's and put the bundles of cane down into the bunk. Those cows were hungry, and they were really eating that feed.

I got that done and drove the tractor around by the granary where we kept it. While it was still running, I took the plug out of the bottom of it to drain the water, then shut it off and went into the house. I was freezing cold! When I got inside, Letia said, "You didn't ask me to use the tractor, and if you ever do that again, I'm going to have the Sheriff come and arrest you and throw you in jail!"

It was always stuff like that! That's what I lived with for several years. The biggest problem was the way she treated me. She'd get mad and wouldn't talk to me. She never did say, "That was a good job you did. Thank you."

I went upstairs, got out of my wet clothes and put on some dry ones. I came back down, and she still wouldn't talk to me. I went outside again and helped milk the cows. I had a little milk stool. (Years later, when I was in that barn, there was my little stool. I wish I could have kept it.)

That's the way much of my life was. She blamed me for a lot and said it was all my fault. Every time anything happened, it was always my fault! She threatened many times to send me back to the orphans' home. (I shouldn't feel this way, but I've gone over this so much that I'm reliving it every day.)

Claude Simmons brought the feed up for the cattle after

that, and I'd have to spread it. Somehow, we got a silo dug down about 26' into the ground. (I don't know who it was that came up and chopped the cane, to make silage and fill the silo.) We used a pulley system to move the feed from the silo to the trough. I had to crawl down into the silo, fill up the box with silage, then climb back up, wind up the box and swing it around to put the silage in the trough. I was so little, I had a hard time getting up on the platform, but if the box was moving, I was strong enough to turn it in the right direction.

————————

I remember when Letia took Maxine and me along with some other kids to see *The Wizard of Oz*. We rode in the back of her pickup to the theater in Quinter, twenty-five miles northeast of Gove. I identified with Dorothy in the story. Just like her, I was searching for "home." The song "Somewhere Over the Rainbow" became popular at that time, and it asked some of the same questions that were in my heart. I dreamed of a land "over the rainbow." I just wanted to fly away (in an airplane) to get away from Letia and find "home." If I could only do that, surely my troubles would be gone. "Somewhere Over the Rainbow" became the theme song for my life as I grew up. My desire for music was born in those years. It seemed like a way to express the loneliness.

After seeing *The Wizard of Oz*, I started thinking of Letia as "The Wicked Witch of the West." With Amos no longer around, Letia made life very difficult for me! I know she was grieving, and it was not easy for her, but I don't know why she had to take it out on Maxine and me.

Letia and the rest of the Blands did not get along very well. She would complain about different ones in the family. Amos' sister and brother-in-law, Aunt Vera and Uncle "Debby" (Delbert) Clothier, would come back from Colorado to visit, but they never would stay at Letia's house. They'd stay at Uncle Cliff and Aunt Ethel's even though it was a basement house. I'd say, "Let's go out there and see them." Letia would tell me, "No, we're not gonna do it." She'd never let Maxine and me go, but we'd sneak off anyway and walk those three miles to get there. Letia seldom wanted to go out to their place.

Maxine was always running out the door with some boy, so I was left at home to listen to Letia. As an escape, I'd sit in front of the radio, (which I now own) and put my hands under my chin while I listened to the songs and stories.

I'd tease Maxine a lot about the boys she went to see. She liked Ralph Anderson. I'd say, "Ralphie, Ralphie, I'm going to come over and see you." That would make Maxine mad, and Letia didn't like it very well either. I had fun doing that. Later, Maxine went with someone who was traveling through with the harvest. She always got together with someone who was a stranger to the community. She was drawn to guys that were from out of town.

Maxine and Uncle Cliff's daughter, Marie, were good friends. They both liked to meet the harvesters who travelled through Gove. One time, Maxine and Marie went walking around town and met up with Ralph and someone else. Marie came with Maxine to spend the night, but they got home late. I stayed awake till they got home then went out into the upstairs hall and stood there leaning over the banister so I could hear what would happen. Letia was awake too, and she whacked Maxine on the legs with Amos' razor strap. Maxine would say, "Hit me again. It didn't hurt." POW, she'd hit her again! "It didn't hurt. Hit me again," Maxine taunted. POW, she hit her again! After about the third time, Maxine said, "Now, you quit that!" POW! "Now, you quit that!" I was standing upstairs hanging onto the railing and laughing. I kidded Marie about that one time, and she said, "I knew better than to get in front of that razor strap!"

SEVEN

DUTY AND HONOR

I wrote the following many years ago:

My life, from the time I can remember, was built on two words. They were Duty and Honor! It was a duty of everyone to perform according to an established set of rules. No love was involved. It was a matter of fact. Go outside of the expected rules and be punished. The form [of punishment] being anything between physical, verbal and shunned. The Honor was really for public opinion. Living in a small community, Honor really meant, don't cause any family embarrassment.

Love: Love was never a part of my life from the earliest time I remember. There was a great vacuum inside which was never filled. I could feel it, a sense of aloneness, longing to be filled.

Life: I remember even at the age of three that something was missing. Although not able to remember my early childhood, there were glimpses or flashes of early youth.

As life began with the Bland family there was someone to play with, "Maxine." I was shown off to all the clan over the months. The Blands were a very clannish people and when they came together blood sealed the unity, not love! I was to learn early that I was a spectator in the family. There were the age-old family stories, the things they liked, the heartaches, and a myriad of their accomplishments. Here again, Duty and Honor prevailed. The Blands never saw fit to adopt me, and so every three to six months a case worker would be around to check on my physical well-being. Being in a small community, it was well known that I was an orphan. When the name calling and laughter from other kids came, it hurt, and when looking for comfort, none came. Duty and Honor did.

EIGHT
UNCLE CLIFF

5-18-1942 We went to the office of Mr. Bland, Sheriff of Gove County and found Don visiting with his uncle...Mr. Bland said that Don frequently visited with him. He was in his brother Amos' home practically every day to help Mrs. Bland with something or to eat lunch with them...

Mr. Bland was of the opinion that Don was a fine boy... Mr. Bland said that Don had not been more difficult for his mother than Maxine since the death of their father.

10-2-1942 We visited with Mrs. Bland alone...Mrs. Bland said that Don had been well. He gets along well in school. Both he and Maxine like their school and their teacher this year. We asked Mrs. Bland if she would like to adopt Don and she said she did not have the extra cash for an adoption. She has tried to pay off the mortgage on the place this year, and it has left her without extra cash. She has even mortgaged the cattle in order to make the payment. We then asked her if she would like to be appointed guardian and explained that it would not be necessary for us to continue to visit but would make her responsible for Don and that she could later adopt him or he could share equally with Maxine by her making a will. She hesitated and rather debated whether she should become guardian or if it would be better for us to continue visiting...she said she had been having trouble with both the children recently...Each of them thinks that she is too hard on them.

Mrs. Bland works outside a great deal; during the harvest she hauled wheat and recently she has helped with the silo filling. She keeps a hired man; the doctor's son is still with them. He began working for them in January because of the stormy weather and has continued to stay since that time. Don dislikes cows and milking...He wants to drive the car and is much interested in tinkering with cars. He has always been interested in mechanical things.

Mr. Bland's brother gave Don an old Ford car. He has rushed home from school each night to work on it and succeeded in tearing it down and rebuilding it. Mrs. Bland is now worried for fear he will get it in running order and want her to furnish gasoline and allow him to drive it.

We discussed with Mrs. Bland the possibility of Don working with one of his father's brothers since he feels that he is grown and perhaps they could teach him to like the farm work. She said he would like to go to the home of the relatives and help them willingly. She could not understand why both children disliked to help in the home. She said Don wanted to tinker with some old machinery, and Maxine liked to read or primp instead of helping with some of the work.

We felt that Mrs. Bland was very much interested in the hired man and wondered if there might be a jealousy on the part of the child. We tried to explain to her that it had no doubt been a shock and very difficult for the children to give up their father. His death had made an unnatural home situ-

ation.[1]

Uncle Cliff was a World War I Army veteran. He served his country and was, at one time, stationed at the Presidio of San Francisco by the Golden Gate Bridge. He was now serving as Sheriff of Gove County.

After Amos died, he spent time with me and made me feel special! Sometimes he'd come up to Letia's and get me, and I'd go with him when he had sheriff duty of some sort. In those days, with Kansas being a dry state, he always had the job of raiding people who were bootlegging, usually north of Highway 40. He'd go up there and come back with his 1941 Ford car sagging from all the whiskey he confiscated, then he'd unload it in the jail behind the Court House. There would be a trial, and most often the guys would be fined and let go, but they lost their booze.

After the judge had passed sentence on them for having whiskey, Uncle Cliff's job was to take the bottles and destroy them. One time, he took me with him out to the Metz place — a small, abandoned limestone house across the road from the home of Aunt Ethel's mother, Anna Johnson. We set the bottles up in the window, and he taught me how to shoot a rifle. We'd do target practice and shoot at all those whiskey bottles. With that strong whiskey in them, they'd just shatter when they broke. You couldn't find a piece of glass as big as your thumbnail. I had a little fun with that. He did too.

At one time, there were two cattle ranchers who were

fighting between themselves over whose cattle were whose. Each one came into the courthouse at certain times and reported the other one. Uncle Cliff had a call from the County Attorney sending him out west of Gove to check things out between those two ranchers. He took me with him, and on the way out, he told me some of the weird things that had happened in Gove County. When we got out to the place where he said we could see the ranchers' houses, we crawled through the buffalo grass in the pasture and up a small knoll, then he said, "Be quiet cause they might hear us." When we got to the top, we could see lantern lights, one coming from one direction and another one farther away. He whispered, "That's them!"

Then he started telling stories about the Fleagle Gang[2] who had robbed a bank in Lamar, Colorado. One member of the gang had been shot, so they came east to Dighton, Kansas, where they tricked a doctor into going with them to treat the wounded gang member. I think they went out north of Healy to a place called Hell's Half Acre. Pretty close to there, they made the doctor take care of the guy who had been shot. When he got done, they shot and killed the doctor, put him in his car, and pushed it into a ravine.

Well, somebody in the Sheriff's Department or the County was smart enough to know that the gang members had rolled the car windows down. They found a fingerprint on one of the windows and sent it to the FBI. The fingerprint belonged to one of the men who had robbed the bank in Lamar. They were eventually caught. Three of them were tried for murder, found guilty and hanged. The fourth one was shot and killed.

He told me more stories, as we were laying there, and finally he said, "Well, I don't think there's going to be anything happening tonight." He stood up and started walking back to the car, and about that time, I knew I'd been had. We didn't need to be quiet and crawl in the grass after all. He was just doing that for the "effect."

Uncle Cliff had quite a sense of humor and liked to pull pranks on people. I think this story was funny, although some people didn't think so at all. He had a pen that looked just like an old-time fountain pen. It was orange and black and had a clip on the side like most pens, but it was really a .38 pistol. It didn't hold a regular shell, but instead held one filled with tear gas. I don't know exactly when he did it, but he went down to the front of the courthouse one day, opened the door and shot that thing off inside the courthouse. Then he stood there with his watch and timed it to see how long it took all those people to get out of there. They were mad at him for some time, but he got a good laugh out of it. I understand that, and I would have laughed too.

He told me his sister, Vera, could ride and shoot better than he or any of his brothers could. She was a fun-loving person. Like Uncle Cliff, she had a great sense of humor.

One time when he went to her house at Sylvia, Kansas, her son wanted to see how his handcuffs worked, so Uncle Cliff handcuffed their two wrists together. When he reached into his pocket to get the key to unlock them, he discovered he had left the key back in Gove. They had to drive 30 miles to Hutchinson to have the handcuffs taken off.

To make me feel important, he told me one day to take

the handcuffs down to the jail cell, put them on the prisoner and bring him up to his office. I was a little apprehensive, but excited to be trusted with such a task. When I got to the cell, I saw that the "prisoner" was just a boy. He had been brought into custody for abusing his sister. He was given the choice of serving a jail sentence or going into the military. He chose to join the military. I believe he was later killed in action.

Around Gove, we heard about a guy who was being tried in court there. Everybody knew about it. A bunch of us boys wanted to go watch the trial. Our manual training teacher, Fred Crippen, took us up there to the courthouse. Those of us who went were Edwin Sanders, Max Wilson, Donnie Crippen and two or three more. We were in the courtroom when all the excitement started. I can still see the defendant. He was a big ol' guy. He had hidden a knife in the sleeve of his long-handled underwear. He got that knife out and was going to stab the lawyer, Harry Thompson. Uncle Cliff started hitting him with his blackjack trying to get the knife away from him. When the fracas was going on, somebody said, "Those kids shouldn't be in here!" I can hear them yet. We were told to get out and were standing in the street when "Mose" (Eldon) Morse, Uncle Cliff's deputy, came down the steps, then turned around and went back upstairs to help. We weren't allowed back in, so that was the end of us watching the action.

When the trial was over, the guy was committed to Larned State Hospital. They said he was insane. Uncle Cliff told me later that as he was taking him down to Larned, the guy said, "Cliff, why don't you take these chains off of me, and when we get to Larned, we'll see if they can tell who the criminal is." Uncle Cliff told him, "No, I can't do that."

There are some stories about Uncle Cliff that I can't tell. He was quite a character. I don't think he ever had an enemy.

———————

Things got worse between Letia and me. We got into an argument one morning, and she told me, "You know you don't belong here! You don't even have a name!" I told her, "I do too, it's Bland!" She repeated, "No, that's not your name. It's not that! You don't have a name, and you don't belong here!" It shocked me so much that I didn't know what to do! She'd already threatened several times to send me back to the orphans' home. That time, it really hit me! I got on my bicycle and rode down to the courthouse to see Uncle Cliff.

I had a hard time riding my bike to his office because I couldn't see through the tears. I went inside the courthouse and up to the Sheriff's Office. I brushed back my tears so nobody would see them, but when I got into his office, I let them go. Uncle Cliff was sitting in his chair. He was so short that when he rocked back, his feet didn't even touch the floor. He was just sitting there rocking back and forth. Now as I look back, I know that he was just waiting. I finally got my composure a little bit and told him the whole story of how Letia said I didn't have a name and that I didn't belong there. He reached over and got a full sheet of paper out of his roll-top desk. With a real flourish, he took a pen and used the whole page to write **B L A N D**. When he got done, he handed it to me and said, "That's your name. I'm giving you mine. I only ask you one thing." I asked, "What's that?" He said, "Don't ever dishonor it." I told him, "I won't do that. I never will." That was the beginning of a real life-change for me. Uncle Cliff cared about me and spent time with me. By investing in my life, he showed me that he loved me.

NINE

THAT BEAUTIFUL BLONDE

One summer, I worked for Letia's brother-in-law, Don Tustin. When he got done cutting his own wheat, we took his tractor and pull-type combine all the way from his place out west of Gove and drove it several miles south of town to cut wheat for his brother, Harlan.

At that time, Harlan and his family were living with his mother, Edith Tustin, in her stone house because a tornado had come through in June 1940 and destroyed Harlan and Lorane's house on the farm. Their daughter, Berniece, was helping her grandma Tustin feed the harvest crew of Lee and Herlin Miller, Don Tustin and myself. When we all stayed there, Berniece slept with her grandma, and I slept in Berniece's bedroom. I remember her bed smelled so good!

Sometime after that, Berniece's grandma moved to Gove. (She lived in the house that was later used as the parsonage for the Gove Methodist Church.) Berniece and her family came to live with her for a while so Berniece could go to high school at Gove. (She had attended grade school at Liberty School east of Harlan's house.)

This is how God works, and I know it to be true! That

fall when high school started, the door opened and there stood that beautiful blonde. I instantly fell in love with her, and my life changed forever. I was a sophomore, and Berniece was a freshman.

The schools had trouble finding teachers in those days, and they'd hire about anybody. There was a Methodist preacher who taught world history. The freshmen and sophomores were put together for that class. All the chairs had a large arm on one side. I always made it my purpose to sit behind Berniece. I'd reach up there and pull some of that golden hair while the preacher was teaching. Berniece would say, "Quit it!" Next time, I'd do it just a little bit more. She said, "Quit it, quit it," and she stood up and stiff-armed me solid! She knocked the chair over with me in it. I was laying there on the floor in the classroom, and everybody was looking at us. She was mad, but she was not embarrassed. I was embarrassed! That was the beginning. From then on, things between us got better. The die was cast.

One time I went to the barber shop in Oakley and got a haircut and bought a big bottle of hair dressing. I remember putting that on my hair, so it'd make it look kinda fussy.

I wanted to have curly hair, and Letia took me to Oakley with her to Menefee's Barber Shop. I got a permanent, and I thought it was pretty nice. When I got back to school, the kids in high school gave me the new nickname "Curly." That nickname stuck, and I carried it all the rest of the time I went to school there.

Roger and Clinton Faubion, Jimmy Scott, Roy Miller, Max Wilson and Leonard Heier were some of my friends at school. Most of them were classmates. They'd say, "Here comes Curly." I was never embarrassed. I thought it was neat. I don't know if Berniece was impressed by it, but she was one of the main reasons I got the perm. When my hair grew out, it really got to be a mess. I didn't have any money to redo it, so we just cut it off.

Berniece confessed that she loved me. In her little memory book that I still have in my bedroom, she wrote something like, "Roses are red, violets are blue, I know you and love you too." I have two of her books like that.

I think it was around a year later when school was out that we parted ways after my junior year of high school and Berniece had finished her sophomore year. Harlan and Lorane moved into a house they had built in Oakley, and of course, Berniece went with them. That was hard for me!

Claude Simmons had built a house for Don Tustin, then he helped build one for Harlan right across the street.

TEN

REJECTED AND SENT BACK

Maxine never helped with the chores. She was in the house and was supposed to be cooking or cleaning. She didn't always do that either, then Letia would come in and have to cook after we had been out doing the chores.

5-24-43 …She [Letia] *said that their greatest difficulty is over the work. Neither of the children are interested in helping as much as she thinks they should...*

From her report it seemed that the children realized they could hurt her feelings and cause her to give up to them by saying cross things to her...

She said that Don is a good worker when he wants to work. His disposition is exceedingly nice excepting when he gets angry about things, that he is perfectly honest, he has never shown any signs of stealing...

We again talked to Mrs. Bland about being appointed guardian for Don, and she did not feel that she was ready for that...

7-1-1943 See letter written by Miss Blanche H. White, State Case Supervisor, in which she asks Mrs. Bland to let the League know whether she plans to some day adopt Don, whether she wishes to be made guardian over him, or if she might sometime return him to the League.[1]

———————

In the summer of 1943, the barn at Letia's burned down and had to be replaced. The new one was built out of rock that came from the Cass quarry west of Gove. I helped load those heavy rocks and could hardly lift them. I didn't go to school for a while until we got enough rock to build that barn. A schoolmate, Bert Summers, had an uncle who was a stone mason. He laid the rock for the new barn. I had to stay home to mix mud for him. He chewed tobacco like you wouldn't believe! I remember that with every rock he laid, he would shape the mortar and then spit tobacco juice on it. I often wondered if someone ever tore that barn down, they'd find a brown spot between every rock.

———————

10-28-43 The family has had so much happen to them this summer...In June the barn was struck by lightning, burning it and several other sheds and outbuildings down. They lost one milk cow also. The pelting rain saved the house from burning. Mrs. Bland said neighbors, friends and relatives had been kind and considerate since these experiences. Mrs. Bland's father is rebuilding some of the improvements. It has all entailed un-

expected expense, worry and hardship. The buildings were not insured.[2]

———————

When I was thirteen, there was a last-day-of-school picnic for all of us at Miles Powers' grove out west of Gove. (I wasn't at the picnic because I went over to Plainville with Hal Fagan, Letia's hired man, to see his mother.)

We heard that the kids had been having fun climbing trees, playing games and giving each other rides from a rope in the hayloft. One person held onto the end of a rope while another would climb up a ladder and jump off making the first person go flying onto the hay stored in the haymow.

They were having great fun until one of the girls, Erma Mae Roemer, climbed up a tree and fell to the ground. She was taken to the hospital in Hays but died from her spinal injury. It was such a tragedy! She was only fifteen.

———————

10-28-1943 Mrs. Bland would not mention Miss White's letter about adopting Don or at least assuming guardianship so we asked her what she planned to do. "I talked…about it and afterwards thought I had really not said what I'd do. You know,…I don't get along with Don. He doesn't like me. Bud (Mr. Bland) could talk with him and tell him to do things and he would willingly, but he won't with me."

If Don could work with a man, Mrs. Bland thinks it would help him more than anything else. She said if we thought it would be better for Don to be in a home with a man she wouldn't stand in his way. We asked if she thought that would suffice and overshadow the fact that this place was home to him and she and Maxine were his folks. She didn't know…

Don threatens to run off and just tells Mrs. Bland he'll pack his own clothes when she offers this service. "You'll go on your own feet and come back on them too, and you'll be <u>glad</u> to get back. Don always says he will <u>never</u> come back…"

Don and Maxine fight and quarrel all the time but stick up for each other when someone else picks on one of them. "I try to be fair but it's hard." The children tell Mrs. Bland on each other. She is trying to train them out of this habit, she said.

"I have my troubles with Maxine, too, though they are different" (from Don's.) "Maxine and I don't agree all the time either."

Once in awhile Don "thrills me so." The other evening when they were walking to the barn he put his arm around her. "He can be so dear when he wants to." We suggested Don possibly loved Mrs. Bland more than she realized and this demonstration was a big step for him to take.

We asked Mrs. Bland if she had discussed the subject of adoption with Don. "He always says he doesn't want to be adopted." We asked if she had talked with him about becoming his guardian and she did not say definitely. We suggested we would talk with Don about the matter. Mrs. Bland, it seemed to us, began to talk faster and was more nervous. We felt she did not want us to stay and see Don…

We asked Mrs. Bland what she expected to do — she had not said definitely. Mrs. Bland finally said she had never thought of or expected to give Don up. This was the only definite statement we could obtain and we brought the subject to focus at least one other time, not related here...[3]

———————

IN THE PROBATE COURT OF GOVE COUNTY, KANSAS

Case No. 1336

In The Matter Of The Petition Of Letia O. Bland, a widow To Adopt Donald Earl, A Minor Child.

PETITION

Comes now this petitioner Letia O. Bland, and for her petition herein states:

That petitioner is a resident and citizen of Gove, Gove County, Kansas; that her post office address is Gove, Kansas, and that Donald Earl, a minor child resides with the petitioner at said herein before named post office address, said minor child having been turned over to the control and custody of the petitioner by the Kansas Children's Home and Service League, an institution authorized under the laws of the State of Kansas, to place children for adoption.

That at the time petitioner received the custody and control of said minor child the only name known to the petitioner of said child was and is Donald Earl; that said Donald Earl was born on the 26th day of October 1929, at a place unknown to petitioner and that he is now Fourteen (14) years of age.

That petitioner desires to adopt said Donald Earl for all in-

tents and purposes as though he were a natural child of the petitioner and that the petitioner has the consent of the said Kansas Children's Home and Service League to adopt said Donald Earl, and that upon adoption of said Donald Earl it is the desire of the petitioner that he, the said Donald Earl, thereafter be known and legally designated as Donald Earl Bland.

That petitioner is the owner of one-hundred and sixty (160) acres of farm land, more or less in Gove County, Kansas, together with a ten room frame house, barn and outbuildings situated thereon where she and said Donald Earl together with Maxine Bland, a natural minor daughter of petitioner reside, of the approximate value of $3,200.00, twenty-six (26) head of cattle and other livestock of the approximate value of $1,400.00 and farm machinery and miscellaneous items of personal property of the approximate value of $1,000.00.

WHEREFORE, The premises considered, petitioner prays for an order of the Court, decreeing that said minor child be adopted by the petitioner; that the name of said minor child be changed to that of Donald Earl Bland, and for such other order or orders as to the Court seems wise and just in the premises.

Letia O. Bland

State of Kansas, County of Gove, SS:

Letia O. Bland, of lawful age, being first duly sworn on oath states that she is the petitioner in the above and fore-going petition in writing; that she has read said petition and subscribed her name thereto and that the matters and statements therein set forth and contained are true and correct.

Letia O. Bland
Subscribed & sworn to before me this 24th day of March '44

L.O. Maxwell (SEAL)
Probate Judge Of Gove County Kansas[4]

———————

3-30-1944 Transfer Summary. Mr. Bland died, and Donald's mother has felt incompetent to assume the responsibility for two adolescent children. She has been approached about the advisability of adopting Don but has never been willing to do so since the death of her husband. It was then suggested that she become Don's guardian, but she was unwilling to assume this responsibility until it was suggested that Don should be taken out of the home if he had no legal status in the group. Mrs. Bland insisted she had never wanted to give Don up, and after considerable correspondence with Miss White, Supervisor, she decided to apply for guardianship if the agency would assume part of the financial responsibility. It was arranged that the agency would pay $10.00 and Mrs. Bland $5…

It is recommended that the worker keep in touch with Mrs. Bland so that she will not forget her agreement to provide for Donald in a legal way. This should not be allowed to ride later than April, in this Worker's opinion.

10-31-1944 …He [County Attorney Linder] *is of the opinion that Mrs. Bland is a driver and works too hard for her own good and that she expects Donald to work as hard as she does and he won't do it. He feels that this caused nine-tenths of their trouble. He states that Mrs. Bland's father, who has a* carpenter shop there in town, gets along very well with the boy and the boy is very fond of him. He has allowed the boy to use his tools and keeps him busy with him part of the time. Mr. Linder also states that Mrs. Bland treats Don as she did when he was a little boy and does not realize he is growing up. She does not want him to do things that other boys his age do. She wants him at home working when he is not in school.

Worker called on Mr. Daniel, [sic] Principal of the high school. He was of the opinion that Don had made great improvement in the last few years, both in his schoolwork and in his attitude…This year he is doing above average schoolwork. He is doing excellent work in manual training and is extremely interested in this type of work. Mr. Daniel states that he feels Don has more responsibilities than the average boy his age. He says that he knows that he milks as many as eight cows and then delivers milk before school in the morning. He feels this is a great deal of responsibility…

1-18-1945 Worker asked Mrs. Bland if she cares as much for Donald as if he were her own son. She hesitated and said "I don't care for him as much as I used to and I think it is because he has acted so terrible in the last few weeks. I can see quite a change in him since Mr. Bland died."

…He doesn't seem to mind working with some of the neighbors and she found that on some days when he refuses to work with her he is working on a neighbor's farm and he seems to really enjoy it. Worker could understand this, as there is a clash between the mother and Donald…

Worker noticed that Mrs. Bland was wearing an engagement (diamond) on her engagement finger and she was not wearing it the last time the worker called. Worker asked her *if she was planning on marrying again and she said that she didn't know, but that she was engaged and the man is in the service. At the present time he is overseas and has been several months. He is the county Doctor's son and a man about her age. She has heard from him recently and if he gets a furlough as he plans, they will probably be married at that time. Worker suggested that this might be one thing that had caused her to feel differently about Donald. She declared that it was not...*

Worker asked Mrs. Bland, do you wish me to take Donald and she would not give worker any direct answer and said, "I don't think that Donald would want to go." Worker said, "It is too bad that you didn't adopt Donald years ago. I feel you would have a different feeling towards him if you had completed the adoption when you should have." She said that it was the Agency's fault, as every time they were ready to adopt, the Agency thought that they should wait until they were more permanently settled. Worker suggested that the Agency was concerned with security of the child and no doubt that the worker who had suggested waiting thought it would be in fairness to you and to the child...Worker explained to her that she had lived in this same locality for at least 4 years and she had been urged during this time to adopt him. Mrs. Bland said she knows that it would be hard on Donald to take him away as he knows no other home, but she thought, that something should be done...She also stated that she did not know that Donald's people were still alive until the report came back from the State Social Welfare Dept. at the time of the first hearing and this was quite a concern to her and she has told Donald this, and that she does not know where his people are from. Worker said that no doubt Donald feels that he has no home in the world, and

*this brings on the feeling that he has no security in her home…
Worker also suggested to Mrs. Bland that all boys at 15 years
were hard to handle…That it takes the patience of a Saint to
deal with them. Mrs. Bland said that Donald is worse than
the usual boy. She stated that she never has any trouble with
Maxine, that she doesn't sass her and she is a hard worker…*

*Worker called at the high school building and talked to Mr.
Daniels the Principal who stated that Donald had done very
good in his high school work the last term, in fact, he made the
highest grade in both English and Geometry of anyone in his
class. He was making out report cards and Donald had 3 A's
and one B. He is a substitute on the basket ball [sic] team and
is taking up the Sax Horn…*

*Mr. Daniels feels that he takes as much responsibility of
home work as any boy his age, however, he said everyone in
town is well aware that he and his mother do not get along…*

Worker asked how he [Donald] *felt about Mrs. Bland pro-
ceding [sic] with the adoption, and he said, if she wanted to,
that it is alright with him…*

*Mr. Linder the county lawyer said that he knew that the
second hearing was past due and he tried to contact Mrs. Bland
and get her in to begin this action, but she didn't seem to be
inclined to start. He said that it was for the worker's own information that everyone in town knew that she was engaged to
Mr. Fagan's son, and that it was his opinion that in all prob-
ability this might have changed her attitude towards Donald.
He stated that he didn't think that Donald was any worse than
any of the boys around there…and that Mrs. Bland was noted
as a fussier [sic] and a fummer, [sic] but that she was also
known for high moral standing and to be a hard worker…He*

is of the opinion that the adoption should take place as soon as possible and Mrs. Bland should do it. Worker said that the final hearing should take place and she had sent the final summary into the state board...

Worker told Mrs. Bland that Donald did not want to leave at the present time and Mrs. Bland said she wasn't surprised at this. Worker said that as long as Donald is going to stay that the final adoption should take place. She said she didn't want this, for then the Agency would be out of the picture and she wouldn't have any authority over Donald. Worker said that we couldn't have the Agency as a threat over Donald. Mrs. Bland said, "After all, that is the only thing that I could say, that I would write to the home and have you take him back." Worker suggested, that no wonder if she said this to him, that he felt as he does toward her. Worker again said that the only solution to the problem and situation is that she proceed with the adoption... Worker also said that she also felt that part of this reaction of Donald's was due to his insecurity and that if the final adoption would take place that he would have a different attitude about the home and the members of the family. Mrs. Bland disagreed with the worker. Worker said that Donald had promised to do better and think twice before he exploded. Worker said that she was very much pleased to know that Donald was doing so well in school...

If Donald had once said that he was willing to leave the home, worker had planned to take him back, but inasmuch as Donald didn't show any inclination to leave, worker didn't feel like insisting that he leave. Mrs. Bland again said that if Donald should leave, and if he does, it will be very hard on him. She didn't once say "I would hate to have him leave and *it would be hard on us." Worker suggested that we would see how things develop since the visit, as Donald had promised to try to do better. Worker suggested that Mrs. Bland not fuss or pick at him and not to be too deeply concerned over his sassing. Worker tried to assure her that he was no worse than lots of boys that the average boy of 15 was extremely sassy and arrogant in his own home. She said, "Well, we'll see…"* [5]

The time came when Letia and I got into an awful argument, and she got so mad that she held to her threats and sent me back to the "orphans' home" when I was fifteen. As near as I could tell, my trouble was that I didn't do enough work, and I backtalked her. When I did do the work, she'd get mad that I didn't do it right. It was just things like that. She expected me to do a man's work, and I couldn't.

The day before I left to go back, someone took a picture of our basketball team in front of the Gove High School building. They put me in the front of the group, and our coach, Oren Daniels, was standing in the back. They had written the date on a basketball. I was holding that, and everyone else was around me. In their way, they were telling me, "Goodbye."

Letia took me to Quinter where we met a lady from the Kansas Children's Home and Service League who took me on to Topeka. A man from Drumm Farm[6] in Independence, Missouri, came to get me and take me there.

---

*2-16-1945 On this date worker called at the Bland home…
There has been the feeling that Mrs. Bland was definitely reject-
ing Donald, partly because of her engagement to Mr. Fagan.
In interview with supervisor it was decided to give Mrs. Bland
a definite time for either completing the adoption or giving the
child up…*

*Mrs. Bland began in her whiny voice that it was going to be
hard to give up Donald but she wanted to do what was best for
the boy and herself. Worker explained to her that we could not
tolerate a situation in which the League was continually used
as a threat, as she is now using us. She admitted this was bad,
but "what am I to do? If I go on with the adoption I know that
he will be just as bad as he ever was, and I will have to call in
the law as I have no control of him…I know he does not love
me and I will admit that since he has acted like he has in the
last several months I do not have the feeling for him that I did
have."*

*…All this time that Mrs. Bland was talking, Donald stood
at the door ready to go to school and did not say a word…*

*Mrs. Bland asked visitor what plan she had for Donald.
Worker explained to her about the Drumm Farm, which was
a home for boys, as possibly the only alternative…Mrs. Bland
said she felt that the separation would be hard on both Donald
and herself, but she felt it was the best for everyone concerned
and yet she just didn't know. She said that if she went ahead
with the adoption she knew she would have trouble, and she
just knew Donald would just pick up and run off…she went
on to say that in a way she hated to give up Donald but she had
definitely decided that Maxine only had one more year in high
school and that she would then be on her own, and if she did*

not adopt Donald she was going to sell her farm and lead her own life. She said she had worked hard all her life and she was tired and that she could do other work away from Gove which would be easier and more profitable. She did not mention her prospective marriage but she cast several glances at her engagement ring and was quite conscious of it…

Worker went to the high school and talked with Mr. Daniels while waiting for Donald's class to be out. Mr. Daniels said Donald was getting along very well and he had had no recent trouble with him. He said that his grades were well up and that he was doing fine work in Manual Training.

Worker met Donald and both went into an empty classroom to talk. Worker showed Donald the catalog of the Drumm Farm…Donald asked worker about his birth certificate and had read a paragraph in the pamphlet which he pointed out to worker that a boy who was an orphan only could go to this home. He said "don't I have some folks?" …Worker explained to him that she was unable to tell him about his family at this time but after he and Mrs. Bland made their decision about what they were going to do she would be able to tell him about his folks.

Worker asked Donald if he wished his mother to continue with the adoption. He said that he did not care, that it was up to her. He said that…Maxine did not like him and threw it up to him lots of times that he was not her brother.

2-17-1945 On this date, at approximately 10:30 A.M., Mrs. Bland called, saying that she had talked with Donald and she had decided that it was best not to go on with the adoption…[7]

3-3-1945 Randels Transfer Summary

…She [Letia] *has had some difficulty with Don and Maxine being impudent and not wanting to help her with the work. It may be that they have been much upset because of the loss of their father…*

He admires his foster father's brother who is sheriff and visits him in his office. We felt that Mrs. Bland was quite interested in the hired man when we visited her last. I wondered if there might not be some jealousy on the part of the children because of her interest in this young unmarried fellow.

She said that he had been very good to her and the children, had worked a part of the time for his room and board, which she greatly appreciated. He is the son of the old doctor in town, and according to her report a well-respected fellow.

Worker visited with Mrs. Bland in Aug. of 1944. Donald was visiting an uncle and was not at home. Mrs. Bland criticized Don throughout the whole interview. She objects to how he spent the $132.00 he earned that summer. However, she admitted that she lacked the knack of disciplining the children…

Worker called again in Oct. 1944…and wanted to learn how Don and Mrs. Bland were getting along. Mrs. Bland was not at home, so worker called at the County Attorney's office and talked with Mr. Linder, and the school principal, Mr. Daniels. Worker learned from Mr. Linder that things were not going so well and that Mrs. Bland did a lot of complaining about Don's behavior also complained that he did not help her with the work as he should. Mr. Linder stated that she was a driver and also a fusser.

Mr. Daniels said that he felt that Don took more responsibility than the average boy of his age. Also that he was doing good work in school.

Worker visited with Don in the Manual Training Room and he was proud to show worker some jewel boxes that he was making for Maxine and his foster mother and some to sell...

Worker received a letter from Mrs. Bland...in which she complained about Don...Worker called on the 18th of Jan, 1945 and Mrs. Bland went on and on and on complaining about Don and that she did not think that she could go on with the adoption...because she feels that if the League had no longer any connection with the case, she would lose control over Don. Worker stated definitely that the League did not like to be used as a threat and that worker was also aware that she was playing the League against Donald and vice versa...

Worker discussed the case with Miss White supervisor, who stated that we should give Mrs. Bland until the 28th of Feb. to make up her mind whether or not she was going to proceed with the final hearing as we would not allow the boy to remain in the home unless some definite action was taken...

On the 16th of Feb. worker called at the home and advised Mrs. Bland that she had come to learn her decision...As worker talked a couple hours with Mrs. Bland and got nowhere, she advised Mrs. Bland that she would expect her to let her know by telephone no later than 10 a.m. the next morning what her definite decision was. She called worker at the appointed time and stated that she was going to have to give him up as she knew she could not handle him if she adopted him. Plans were made to make application for Donald at the Drumm Farm.

Worker received a letter from the Shawnee Red Cross Chapter stating that his brother Marion, who was in the Navy, wished to write to Don. Worker received a wire from Mr. Nelson of the Drumm Farm on March 1, 1945 stating that he would accept Don. Worker called Mrs. Bland and told her to have Don ready that worker would be after him Friday the 2nd of March. Worker brought Don to Hays and had a complete physical by Dr. L. W. Reynolds. He stated that he was in fine physical condition and a very clean fellow.

We arrived at the Drumm Farm, Sat. March 3rd at 6 p.m.[8]

IN THE PROBATE COURT OF
GOVE COUNTY, KANSAS.

In the Matter of the Petition of	)	
Letia O. Bland, a widow, to adopt	)	*Case No. 1336*
DONALD EARL SHUGART,	)	
a Minor Child.	)	

APPLICATION TO DISMISS
ADOPTION PROCEEDINGS

Comes now the Kansas Children's Home and Service League, a child-placing agency of Topeka and Wichita, Kansas, and shows to the court that the petitioner, Letia O. Bland, no longer desires to adopt the said Donald Earl Shugart and has returned the said Donald Earl Shugart to the custody of your applicant, the Kansas Children's Home and Service League, which has consented to said return and accepted the actual custody, care and control of the said Donald Earl Shugart.

WHEREFORE, the premises considered, applicant prays for an order of the court dismissing the petition for adoption herein, and decreeing that no final order of adoption be issued in said matter and that the said Donald Earl Shugart be returned to the actual care and custody of the Kansas Children's Home and Service League, under the name of Donald Earl Shugart.

THE KANSAS CHILDREN'S
HOME AND SERVICE LEAGUE,

By Benj. F. Hegler
Its President

STATE OF KANSAS   ) ss.
SEDGWICK COUNTY.   )

Benj. F. Hegler, of lawful age, being first duly sworn, states:

That he is the President of The Kansas Children's Home and Service League, and that he has signed the above and foregoing application, as such president; that he has read said application and that the facts therein stated are true.

Subscribed and sworn to before me, the undersigned Notary Public this 6th day of March, 1945.

Notary Public
My Commission expires April 24, 1948.

———————

APPROVAL

The attached, within and foregoing application is hereby and on this _____ day of March, 1945, approved by the undersigned, Letia O. Bland, who hereby relinquishes to The Kansas Children's Home and Service League, the care, custody and control of the said Donald Earl Shugart. The undersigned also waives all notice of the hearing upon said application.

Letia O. Bland
Witness:[9]

March 5, 1945
Re: Case No. 1336
Probate Court of Gove County, Kans.
Adoption of Donald Earl Shugart

Mr. Jesse I. Linder,
Attorney at Law,
Gove City, Kansas.

Dear Mr. Linder

I am returning herewith the petition to dismiss the adoption proceedings, which you sent me. I have not signed this petition because I am advised that the facts are not true. I am also advised that the real reason why Mrs. Bland wants to get rid of this boy, is that the man to whom she is engaged to marry does not want the boy.

I very seriously object to any facts being found by the court which in any way reflect upon the character of this boy, as he is in no sense a problem child and is very tractable and manageable. His school record is excellent.

However, as you state in your letter, the League has taken him back from Mrs. Bland, and it is the desire of the League that the adoption proceedings be dismissed. Therefore, I have prepared the application which you will find enclosed and which I would like to have approved by Mrs. Bland and signed by the court. I also enclose a form of final order which I have approved.

We do not want anything to go into the record which reflects on this boy, and I do not think it is necessary that the reasons for the cancellation of the adoption proceedings be set out in the application. The mere fact that the adoptive parent has changed her mind, is a sufficient reason for cancelling the adoption proceedings. It would be a great mistake to go ahead with them, even though she might not have any good reason for the position which she has taken.

Very truly yours,
Benj. F. Hegler
Enc.[10]

3-8-1945 Transfer Case to Topeka. On this day, Mr. Nelson of the Drumm Farm called worker stating that Don had taken a spell of home sickness last evening and said that he would like to go back to that part of the country and that he could get a job on the farm out there. He also said that before he left that Mrs. Bland said that if he would behave himself, she might give him another chance and he thought that this might be possible. Mr. Nelson said that he was a fine boy, is a good student, and had started in school well and he hated to see him leave, as he felt that he had a future but he did not want him to feel that he had to stay if he was not happy...Mr. Hegler stated that...we had the boy in our possession and... there would be nothing against the boy shown in the petition. Worker had a letter from Mrs. Bland dated March 7, 1945 and she asked again for Don's address as she had his dirty clothes washed and ready to send to him. She also asked about Don's ration books...Donald came to Topeka as arranged on Saturday morning. Arrangements were made for him to stay with Mr. and Mrs. Johnson at Emmett, Kansas for the week-end and perhaps a few days longer if necessary. It seemed to me to be necessary to clear up the situation between Donald and his mother before any further plans could be made for him which he would accept because he had the idea that his mother would take him and we knew from Randels' talk with her that she did not want him. I, therefore, called Mrs. Bland on the phone and made arrangements for her to come to Topeka on Wednesday so that we could settle the situation. Mrs. Bland objected and did not want to be put in a position of having Donald blame her for sending him away from home. I insisted, however, that she come as that was the only way we could straighten out the matter and Donald was wanting to return to her home. Mrs. Bland came in on the Union Pacific which arrived here early Wednesday morning. I talked with her alone in the office. She was constantly trying to put me on the defensive and demanded some explanation as to why she had to be here…I tried to clear up the matter of whether she did want him back or not. She repeated that she could not have him back with his behavior what it was and we discussed whether or not his behavior could change. She said she thought he would not change, he would always be the same, and she would not take him back unless he did change. However, she did not want to tell him that, I felt.

I finally said that I thought we could not do anymore until I talked with Donald. A little later Donald came in the office from Emmett. I talked to him alone for a minute or two and then called his mother in. I opened the conversation by saying that Donald had wanted to go home and that he was sure his mother would take him back if he would behave himself. From there on Donald and Mrs. Bland carried on the conversation which usually developed into an argument about whether Donald did something or not. Donald pointed out that Mrs. Bland's daughter had been doing the same things he had… but got by with it. Mrs. Bland insisted that she had not… In the morning when I had mentioned their hired man and mentioned Mrs. Bland's getting married again, she had become very defensive and had told me that this was not the reason she had sent Donald away…She insisted that this had nothing to do with the situation. Donald brought it up in his talk with his mother and she became defensive again, saying that it had nothing whatsoever to do with the situation…

I tried to bring out in this interview the fact of Mrs. Bland's real feelings about having Donald returned. I tried to verbalize for him the things he had been feeling through the years and he had not been able to say in words, such as the fact that if a child is really accepted in the home as a son, then there is no question of sending him away for such misbehavior as Donald had shown. Also, that if she really wanted Donald as her son, she would take steps immediately to complete the adoption and in fact would have completed it much sooner even though she said she had been advised by the agency to postpone adoption when she first took Donald. I pointed out that her feelings for Donald as a son and her desire to have him as her son apparently were not strong enough to overcome other resistances that she could set up. Mrs. Bland did not come out in so many words and tell Donald that she did not want him anymore. However, it was apparent to her and to me from her answers to what I said that this was the situation.

After this interview, I talked with Donald alone. One of his first reactions was that he knew now that the man she is intending to marry did not want him. It was interesting that he had gotten this from her attitude and not from what she said because her words were directly opposite. He said he had suspected this all along and now he was sure of it. I tried to get him to say that he would let Mrs. Bland go back to Gove and he would take his chances with the League as to what plan we could make for him.

As I talked with Donald at this time, I felt it would be better for him to give up the idea of returning to Mrs. Bland's home completely before we discussed any further definite plans. I felt this was true especially if Mrs. Bland did not want him in her home and that that relationship should be clarified in his mind before he went back to the community, if he should go. However, Donald was too insecure and hesitant to be able to say that he could give Mrs. Bland up completely. He realized that he could not live with her if she did not want him. However, *he was fearful of taking his chances with the League. He asked what kind of a home we would find for him and I told him probably one similar to the place where he had been staying for the last few days. He asked if he would be adopted, and I told him no, probably not, that he was pretty old now to be adopted and that usually when people wanted to adopt children they took younger children, usually babies. Donald did not want to be adopted. He had appreciated the fact that I had addressed him by letter at the Johnson's as Donald Bland instead of Donald Shugart.*[11]

ELEVEN

RESCUED BY "DAD"

It was told to me later that Uncle Cliff, Aunt Ethel and their kids were sitting at their table eating supper when Wayne said, "Well, we won't be seeing Don anymore." Uncle Cliff asked, "What are you talking about?" He said, "Oh, Letia sent him away."

One night as they were laying in bed after Letia got rid of me, Uncle Cliff and Aunt Ethel were trying to figure out what they could do to help. They decided they were going to complete what Amos started. They agreed that they would give me a home and treat me as their own son.

A lot of things happened in the next two weeks. I don't know how, but they did. Letia would not tell Uncle Cliff and Aunt Ethel where I was. Jesse Linder, the County Attorney, found out that I was down in Independence, Missouri, at a place called Drumm Farm. It was not a happy place for me! I wasn't sure what was going on. It seemed to me that rich people would come get their kids on the weekends and take them home like they were toys then bring them back out at the beginning of the week. On the weekend, I was there by myself with the little kids, and I had to go to bed when they did. I just couldn't take it! The bed was even too small for me.

I told the man in charge I wanted to go back to west Kansas and that if he didn't let me go, I would go across the pasture and get on the train that was moving through the valley. He got mad, said a few things that weren't good and told me I'd never amount to anything! He called the Children's Home in Topeka and told them he was sending me back. A guy drove me up to the front of the bus depot in Independence, and said, "Get out!" I did, and he drove off. He didn't give me a ticket or anything.

I had some money from selling a desk that I had made in the manual training class at Gove High. Jimmy Scott bought it for twenty-seven dollars. I rat-holed the money so nobody knew I had it. I used fourteen dollars to buy a Greyhound Bus ticket to Topeka.

The lady at the Kansas Children's Home and Service League asked me what I wanted to do. I told her I wanted to go back to west Kansas. She had Letia come to Topeka, and I told her I'd change if I could just go back with her. Letia said she didn't think I had changed. We got into an argument, and the social worker said, "That's all we need. We will not let you go back with her!" Letia left, and I asked, "So what am I going to do now?" She said they couldn't send me back to West Kansas because they didn't have anybody to send me back to, but they would find a place for me to go.

I was in Topeka about three days, then they sent me to Emmett, Kansas, north of St. Marys, and I stayed with a couple for about a week.

Uncle Cliff called down to Topeka and talked to the people at the Children's Home and said he'd like to have me come live with him. They asked me if I knew I had an uncle who wanted me, and I couldn't figure out who it would be. I thought maybe it was Uncle Don Tustin. I didn't know of any other uncles who would want me. She finally said, "Well, it's Cliff Bland." I said, "Why does he want me? He's got five kids of his own!" She said, "He wants you!"

So, he and Wayne rode the train down to Topeka. The man from the Kansas Children's Home and Service League brought them out to Emmett to pick me up. When they came for me, I was elated! I looked up, and my heart did a flip because they were people I knew, and they cared for me! I knew Uncle Cliff was holding to his promise to give me his name. The man turned me over to him, took us to Saint Marys where all three of us got on the train and headed west. We rode all the way to Grainfield where Aunt Ethel met us at the depot.

Wayne was always my friend. The two of us had talked to each other a lot. After school, while waiting for his dad to get done with his work at the Sheriff's Office, he'd come up to Letia's. He'd never come inside, but he and I would go out and feed the cattle or something, and we'd just sit down and talk. We were very, very close! I don't know how to explain it any other way.

At that time when my uncle Cliff, for whom I was so grateful, came and rescued me and brought me back to live in his home on the farm three miles northwest of Gove, in my eyes and in my heart, he became my dad! When asked about my foster dad, Cliff Bland, I threw the "foster" away a long time ago! He was "Uncle Cliff" for years, and then he was "Dad." He and Aunt Ethel truly became Dad and Mom to me. I didn't remember my own mother, so I wasn't able to call her "Mom." Since I had no memory of my father, and I wasn't allowed to get very close to Amos, Cliff Bland was the only man I ever considered to be a dad to me.

———————

3-8-1945 Transfer Case to Topeka [Continued] *...previous to our talk with Mrs. Bland, Donald's uncle from Gove had asked the County Attorney there to call, saying that he wanted Donald and would be glad to take him in his home, if that could be arranged. He said he had not known that Donald was going to leave the community or he would have asked for Donald at that time. This uncle is Mr. Clifford Bland. He said that he would be glad to come to Topeka for Donald if we should want him to do so.*

...I told him [Donald] *that his uncle, Cliff Bland, in Gove, wanted him to come to live with him and had said he would come to Topeka for him if we wanted him to. I told him his uncle had also said he did not know that he was leaving or he would have made plans before that. Donald was surprised that this uncle wanted him. He had thought that it would be Mrs. Bland's brother* [brother-in-law] *whom he calls Uncle Don. However, he had said that Uncle Don is leaving the community. After I had told him this about his uncle he was silent for a moment and then he said, "Well, I did not know he thought that much of me." I told him that his Uncle Cliff would not adopt him but he was willing to take legal guardianship of him,*

which meant that his Uncle Cliff would stand in the same relation to him that the League had been standing all these years. I said that I thought it would be better for it to be that way than for Donald to have someone from the League coming into the community often to inquire how he was getting along, etc. I had mentioned this before to Donald as it seemed to be something he resented very much. Donald at this time commented that he wasn't saying but he had his own opinion about such visits. I said that I knew he had and I thought I knew how he felt about it. He grinned and said, "Yes, I think you do but I'm not saying."

I tried to get Judge Linder, County Attorney, long distance before Donald had to leave to return to the Johnson home with them but was not able to do so. Therefore, I told Donald that I would call and let him know as soon as I had word about his uncle coming for him. Donald said that he could go by himself all right. He returned to the Johnson home. A little later I talked with Judge Linder. Judge Linder was very understanding of what the situation was in regard to Donald's feelings about the matter. He told me that Mr. Bland would be willing to come to Topeka for Donald. I said that I thought it would mean a lot to Donald if he did that. Mr. Linder said that that was the reason it was suggested because he too felt that it would mean so much to Donald to have his uncle come for him. He said it had been suggested that it would be easier for the boy to come on the train but because of Donald's feelings, it was decided that Mr. Bland would come in. Mr. Linder was to get in touch with him and let me know later exactly when he would be here, and I learned later that Mr. Bland expected to arrive on the Union Pacific early the next morning.

On Thursday morning when Mr. Bland and his son came in, I called the Johnsons and told Donald that his uncle was in town and that we would be out for him in the car. Mr. Bland and his son went with me to Emmett where we picked up Donald. Donald was very glad to see his uncle but was quite serious about the situation because we had been delayed by the mud and it was so late. I left Donald and his uncle and Wayne at St. Marys to take the train west from there. I told Donald that I would write him sometime later about the guardianship proceedings.[1]

TWELVE

A HOME WITH DAD AND MOM

I didn't know what was going to happen, but Dad and Mom were good to their word and took me in like a son. Mom turned out to be a very good mother. She was quite the historian. She was half Swede and was proud of her heritage. I'm glad she was!

There were times that she'd get on a rampage, and Dad would say, "Whoa, whoa, whoa." She'd just settle right down. (You've got to remember the Bland boys were horse people.) Dad and Mom got along very well. I could feel their love for each other.

I went back to school at Gove for my junior year. Whenever something special happened in high school, Mom would be there to support me. In those days, they didn't cook meals at school. We brought our own lunches. When we were getting ready for our junior banquet, she helped in the kitchen. In my mind, I can still see her as I looked through the door of the home ec. room. She'd be in there scrubbing carrots or something. She didn't ask me, she just came. She was always there for me! When I was in the junior play, I had one of the lead roles, and she was proud of me.

I remember one of Aunt Vera and Uncle "Debby's" visits to the farm. They had a daughter, Vida, who was just a few inches taller than a midget. When they drove into the yard and got out, Dad walked over, picked her up and carried her around like a baby. She got so mad! She wanted him to put her down, but he wouldn't for a little bit. He got a big kick out of that.

———————

Wayne was learning to drive the car about that time. He was trying to drive it into the center section of the granary, and Dad was directing him away from the sides. Wayne got too close and rubbed the chrome on the side. Dad just calmly said, "Now Waynie, you've got to get over a little bit, so back it out." Before Dad could direct him, he drove it in again and rubbed the other side. Dad said, "Now Waynie, you've got to watch both sides when you put the car in the granary." I thought, "Only Wayne could get away with that!"

Dad and Mom decided to build a house on top of their basement home. They got limestone blocks from the Cass quarry southwest of Gove. Dad went to Grinnell and bought a truckload of old railroad ties. He, Clifford and some neighbors jacked the roof up little by little and criss-crossed the ties on top of each other at each corner of the basement to hold the roof as they built the rock walls up.

While the house was being built, Dad, Mom, Marie and Elinor slept in the limestone brooder house that had been cleaned and whitewashed for that purpose. Clifford, Wayne and I slept in the granary. We were in the center alleyway on Army cots that Dad got for us. (Before that time, Clifford, Wayne and I had slept in the attic of the basement house on those Army cots.)

We had chickens in one of the grain bin sections on the south side of the granary. We kept them there so we could find and gather their eggs. The north side had grain stored in those three bins.

Mom had a gas-powered washing machine. She had two washtubs full of water, one with soap and one to rinse, and she was having me empty them or something. Clifford was using a coffee can to fill the little one-horse engine with gasoline. The gas tank was underneath the engine, and he had to fill it through the spokes of the flywheel. I was right beside the engine while Clifford was doing that, and he spilled a lot of gasoline in the process. Some of it got on me and some spilled on the ground. When he cranked that thing up, it set the ground on fire and me too.

I took off running toward the pasture gate west of the granary. It was open, and I was "mobiling!" I could hear Dad say, "Lay down, lay down, lay down!" I didn't do it, because all I could think to do was run! I was almost to the gate when Clifford tackled me, and Dad was right behind him. Dad jumped astraddle of me and started trying to put the fire out by beating it with his straw hat, but when he looked down, my hide was coming off with it. He stopped beating the fire and instead just held his hat there and was able to smother the flames.

The fire burned my legs and my side. I think Clifford

was taking my boots off. The thing I remembered later is that there were two washtubs full of water and another tub full of wet clothes, and I passed right by all of them as I ran away.

A neighbor, John Powers, drove Mom and me to the hospital in Quinter. His car quit on the way, and a local farmer came along and took us the rest of the way. I had clean underwear on because Mom made sure of that, but no other clothes. I had only a bedspread wrapped around me.

The doctor and nurses looked at the burns, and they were busy doctoring them. I was just laying there. When they finally got me bandaged up, they told Mom to take me home and come back a few days later. After I'd seen the doctor, I wouldn't go out through the lobby because I still didn't have on any clothes except my underwear. They put that bedspread back around me, and we went out the back door. By that time John Powers was there to take us home.

When we got back to the farm, they moved me out of the granary and put me in the brooder house so I could be close to Mom if anything happened. I guess I was delirious all night long, and who was there holding my hand but Mom.

For a while after that, I couldn't even wear underwear because it would rub my skin. I had on a pair of overalls that didn't rub. It wasn't very fun because I needed to have some more clothes on, but I didn't know what to wear. The burn left a big scar on my side.

———

Dad and Kenneth bought a quarter section of ground across the road to the east of Grandma Johnson's house while Kenneth was away in the Army. Dad was sick at the time, but I didn't know just how bad he was. Because of his poor health, Clifford and I broke out that ground so we could get rid of the grass and use it for farmland. I would plow at night because the tractor had lights on it. If I paid attention, I could keep the plow in the furrow and not leave any grass standing. That's what I tried to do. There's a draw that runs right down through the middle of the quarter. It was hard to plow because I'd have to go over it two or three times to break up that sod.

When I drove the tractor to the house in the morning, Clifford would take it out and plow during the daytime. Clifford didn't like it because I'd come in from the field and go to bed. He'd have to put fuel in Dad's Case tractor and go out to work. One time he tried to get me to go down to milk the cows, but Dad told him that I'd been working all night, and I could go to bed. He told Clifford to go milk the cows like he was supposed to. Clifford didn't like that very much.

Topeka, Kansas,
July 12, 1945

Mr. Clifford Bland,
Gove, Kansas.

Dear Mr. Bland:

I am wondering if you would be ready at this time for us to start the necessary procedure to change guardianship of Donald from our agency to you. This was the thing we had talked about previously, I believe. I had the feeling at that time, and I think you did also, that it would be better for Donald to have the authority in regard to his plans come from you instead of from our agency. If we continue with our guardianship, it would mean that someone from here would have to be coming into the community every once in a while to see how Donald is getting along. I believe that Donald has not liked this in the past and I can certainly understand his viewpoint.

I hope that things are going well for both of you. If it is your desire that we proceed with these plans for change of guardianship, will you please let me know. Perhaps you will be willing to show this letter to Donald and you and he can talk the matter over and let me know what you wish me to do next.

Very truly yours,
(Miss) Marjorie Foulke
Acting State Case Supervisor
MF:b[1]

———

Topeka, Kansas
July 19, 1945

Mr. Benj. F. Hegler

411 Brown Bldg.
Wichita, Kansas

My dear Mr. Hegler:
Re: Donald Shugart

You will probably recall having some correspondence with Miss Foulke about the case of Donald Earl Shugart. Your letter of March 5, 1945 addressed to Mr. Jess [sic] I. Linder, Attorney at Law, Gove City, Kansas, was in regard to dismissing the adoption proceedings in this case. Subsequent to that time Donald was placed in the home of Mr. Clifford Bland of Gove City, Kansas. He has apparently made a very nice adjustment in this home and we believe that the guardianship of this boy should be transferred to Mr. Bland.

I am writing to ask that you prepare the proper papers and we will go ahead with the proceedings. I am enclosing a copy of Miss Foulke's letter to Mr. Bland and also a copy of Mr. Bland's reply.

If you need other information in regard to this boy in connection with this transfer of guardianship, I shall be glad to supply it for you.

Very truly yours,
(Mrs.) Leila N. Myers,
Case Supervisor, Topeka
LNM:v
Encl.[2]

Kenneth met Mae in Mobile, Alabama, while he was stationed at Brookley Field Air Base where she worked as a "Rosie the Riveter." They dated for two months and decided to get married. They were married only eleven days when he was shipped out to go overseas. After the announcement of V-J Day, Mae turned in her tools and came to Kansas. She rode the train to Kansas City then boarded a bus to Grainfield. We had no phone at the farm, so she called Letia, who went to Grainfield, picked her up from the depot and brought her out. Kenneth had sent a picture of her to the folks. Dad was such a character, that when she got out of the car, he greeted her by asking, "Where have I seen that mug before?" Little did she know what would take place the very next day as he was teaching her to drive the car.

THIRTEEN

MY WORLD WAS SHATTERED...AGAIN!

Dad had terrible headaches for quite some time and couldn't do much work. I remember he would put big cotton swabs with medicine on them up his nose to try to clear his sinuses. When he'd take the swabs out, they would be bloody, but he could breathe a little better for a while.

He would have to go to bed when he'd have one of his headaches. Mom used to say she always knew when he was feeling better because as she walked by the bed, he would reach out and pinch her.

I'll never forget the day of August 27, 1945!

Clifford and I were rounding up the horses from the north pasture so we could ride. (My horse was the one Don Tustin had given me when I was younger.)

Clifford was quite a horseman. He was kinda rough with them, but he did know how to handle horses. I was holding the gate open so they would go down the drive and into the corral as he drove behind them with the car. We just got them through the gate when Mom came out of the house flapping her apron to get our attention. She said, "Put them back in the pasture! Dad has had a stroke! He's in Quinter, and I'm going right over."

Tragedy struck again! — Dad died before Mom was able to get there.

It was less than six months since Dad had come to rescue me. I was fifteen.

Again, my world crashed down around me! My dad, Cliff Bland, who had given of his time when I so needed him, had given me his name, had rescued me, had taken me into his home and loved me as his own son, the only man I ever felt close to as my father…was…gone! He meant so much to me. All I could think about was that all those things he had done for me and the time he had spent with me was suddenly over. His death was a huge shock, and I was devastated!

———————

The local newspaper article read:

"Cliff Bland Died Very Suddenly Monday Night"

Suffered Paralytic Stroke While in His Car at About 6:30 p.m. Died Quinter Hospital 8:00.

Funeral services for Cliff Bland are being conducted at Gove Methodist Church at 2:00 this afternoon. At the time this is written (early Thursday morning) it is said no word has yet [sic] *from a son Pfc. Kenneth Bland out at Manila, whom the Red Cross has been trying to locate.*

Cliff Bland, 48, died suddenly at the Quinter hospital Monday evening following a paralytic stroke which occurred only an hour and a half before. With his family he had lived on a farm about two miles northwest of Gove.

Cliff and his daughter-in-law Mrs. Kenneth Bland and two of his children Wayne and Elinor were driving from Gove to their farm home at a little after 6:30 o'clock Monday night. Mrs. Kenneth Bland was driving. Cliff also was in the front seat. When they were about a half mile from town Cliff complained of a sharp pain in the back of his head. Shortly after that he slumped over against the driver.

Nick Malsom, a farmer who lives west of Gove, was working in a field near the road. Wayne Bland called for him to come to the car. When he saw Cliff's condition Nick drove the Bland car to the Dr. Fagan home where the doctor said Cliff was in a serious condition and should be gotten to a hospital at once.

Co. Sup't. Chas. Johnson, who was on highway 23 returning to Gove, volunteered to take the sick man to the Quinter Hospital. Mrs. Kenneth Bland went along. At Grainfield Charley stopped to phone the hospital, telling them the particulars and stated he would be at the hospital as quickly as possible. Clem Reitcheck of Grainfield accompanied Charley to Quinter to be of assistance. At Quinter Clem Reitcheck and "Spot" Miller carried Cliff into the hospital. And a half hour later — at 8:30 — the end had come.

Wayne and Elinor Bland went home and told their mother, and she drove to Quinter at once.

From Quinter Charley Johnson drove to Grinnell to ask John Borah of the local Red Cross to try to contact Cliff's son Pfc. Kenneth Bland who is in Manila to learn if he could arrange to come to the funeral. The Red Cross gave much encour-

agement and thought it possible that Kenneth might get home.

For two terms Cliff served as sheriff of Gove County. He was elected in 1938 and re-elected in 1940. His tenure of office was from the first part of 1939 to the first part of 1943.

He was active in the affairs of the local American Legion. He helped organize Geo. M. Scott Post 301 Gove and was always ready to do his part in meetings, at the Decoration Day parade, at the bingo stands or in any other capacity where his services were needed.

Surviving are his wife Ethel; the three sons, Pfc. Kenneth Bland of Manila and Clifford Jr. and Wayne of the home; also two daughters Marie and Elinor, both of the home.

Cliff was preceded in death by his parents and by three brothers, Jean, Amos and Ross. He is survived by a sister Mrs. Delbert (Vera) Clothier of Wichita, KS., and by a brother Forest of Holly, Colorado.

Our community has lost a good citizen and the sympathy of all is with the family in this sorrowful hour.[1]

A portion of his obituary reads:

Into this home circle five children, Clifford Jr., Kenneth, Marie, Elinor, Wayne and Don who was welcomed into the family fellowship as a youth.

———————

I continued with school that fall at Gove High. I knew Mom had a tremendous load on her shoulders after Dad died. Kenneth was away in the Army serving in the Pacific, and Marie had just started teaching at Liberty School six miles southeast of Gove.

Mae started working on the B-29s at Walker Air Base east of Hays. She rode down to Walker with Ralph Hunter, the uncle of my schoolmates, Roger and Clinton Faubion.

I think it was a couple of months later when the news of Dad's death finally reached Kenneth. It was hard to contact him because he was moving from place to place in the Pacific on an aircraft repair ship.

Clifford, Elinor and Wayne were still at home. Things were very, very rough. Mom was trying to get the house finished that Dad had started building. She hired their friend, Andrew Anderson, to do most of the work on it.

I worked for a couple of weeks during harvest for Allen Beesley ("Big Foot") driving the tractor pulling the combine. When we got done with harvest, I came back and helped Clifford put in the sewer line for the house.

FOURTEEN
MARIE AND THE CAR

On Halloween night, we were going to go to Gove to see what was going on.

Marie got a ride from Missouri Flats to Gove with Lee Miller, who lived on Harlan Tustin's old place. (Lee's dad, Herlin Miller, was Harlan's hired man.) Marie had contacted me and said she wanted to use the car. I had asked Mom if I could drive it to town. She said, "You can take it, but don't let anything happen to it because that's the only car we've got. The pickup isn't running." I said, "Thank you. When I get to town, I'll probably just park it and be with Len Heier."

When I saw her in town, Marie said, "I want the keys to the car." I said, "You can't have them. Mom said we can't drive it all over the place or let anything happen to it." Marie talked me into giving her the keys. The reason she wanted the car was so she and Maxine could rope outhouses. Because we had a lot of horses, we had lariats in the car. They would throw the lariat around the toilet, tie the other end to the bumper of the car, take off and pull it over. They were having quite a good time!

Several kids put culverts and other stuff on Main Street and did things like that. Someone took some milk goats and put them on top of a haystack. They would get in trouble and have to put everything back.

I had other things on my mind…my girl. There was a guy who had an old-time truck with wooden wheels. All of us guys would take our girlfriends and ride in the back on alfalfa bales while he drove us all around. Berniece and I sat in the back of the truck with quite a few other couples. We liked to go under the bridge on the Hackberry. You couldn't get out of the vehicle because the bridge was so narrow. We had fun just riding around and doing a little smooching.

When we got ready to go home, there sat Mom's car on Main Street, and smoke was coming out from under it. I asked Marie, "What did you do to the car?" She said, "Oh, nothing. It's a leak in the exhaust system. Don't worry about it, just take it home." When I got the car home, Mom was there, and she saw the smoke. She said, "What did you do?" I said, "Nothing." I didn't tell her that Marie had had it because of that "secret trust" thing. Mom didn't say much, but she never "saw me" for the next week. I could sit at the table, and she would not talk to me.

Marie would come home on weekends from teaching. She got a ride home, and I knew she was coming. When I saw her, I ran out the front door and said, "None of the family, Mom, Clifford, Elinor nor Wayne has talked to me all week because of the car." She said, "Don't worry. I'll take care of it." She went inside and told Mom, "I was the one driving the car, Don wasn't." When I walked in, everybody "saw me" again. I wasn't invisible anymore.

Marie paid for the car repairs (a new muffler) out of her school wages. I never asked for the car after that. I didn't blame Mom for being upset. That's the only car she had, and she needed it.

FIFTEEN
ON MY OWN

After my junior year of high school, in May of 1946, I decided I needed to set out on my own. All I could see was that Mom was trying to get me through school, but she had her other kids to care about. She didn't need the extra burden of caring for me. I said to myself, "Don, go so she can get these kids educated."

I sold my horse at the sale barn in Oakley. I knew I had to leave to find work, so I got a ride up to Grainfield. I think Fred Crippen took me. I got in a boxcar on the train heading west. Some man was in the shadows as I was standing in the doorway, and he said, "Hey, where ya goin', fella?" I just about jumped out of that boxcar! He was a bum-looking guy. I said, "I'm following the harvest." He asked, "Well, why don't you just stay with me, and we'll both harvest." I told him, "I'm getting off at this next town to find out whether I can get work or not." Oakley was coming up, and I got off there.

Maxine was working in a restaurant at the filling station on the south side of town. She put in a good word for me, and I got a job pumping gas at that station. The owner had bought some military equipment, jeeps and motor scooters. Since I had rented a room up town that cost me $4.00 a month, I bought a motor scooter from him so I could ride back and forth to work. I hadn't worked there very long when the man sold the station, so Maxine and I both lost our jobs.

Dick Farmer owned the grocery store in Oakley. I went to work stocking shelves for him. One day I looked up, and there was Mom. She had come to town to shop. We talked a little bit, and she said, "I need some soap to wash clothes." There wasn't any on the shelves, so I told her, "There's some downstairs. I'll get it for you." I put it in a sack, gave it to her, and she put it in her cart. When Mom went to check out, the cashier told Mr. Farmer what I had done.

He called me to the back of the store, and said, "You weren't supposed to give that. We don't have much of it, and I'm the one who gives it away. You're out of here!" That cost me my job. I started to go out the front door, and he said, "No, you go out the back door." I went out that back door and walked up the alley. When I got around to the north side of the building, there was Mom loading her groceries into the car. She asked, "What are you doing out here?" I said, "I got fired."

The next job I had was to work for Arden Numer who had a contract with the Union Pacific Railroad to unload freight from box cars. In those days, we didn't have forklifts. I was little for my age, and that was hard work. When we had bricks to unload, we used brick handles to pick up six bricks at a time. Mr. Numer also had me help shovel sand. That's a very hard job!

The REA (Rural Electrification Administration) had come into Logan County, and they started shipping creosote telephone poles. To unload them, we'd pick up one end, put it over the side of the railroad car and let it roll off. I ruined my clothes with the creosote.

After working for Mr. Numer, I got a job with a Mr. Sellers who lived in the north part of Oakley. I helped him rehab a house. We took the lath and plaster off the walls and replaced that with sheetrock. He liked me, and I learned that trade right there in that house.

When September came around, Mom said I had to come home, finish my senior year, and get my diploma. I rode my scooter to Gove to talk to her about it.

Mom was at Grandma Johnson's house, so I went over there and told her, "I came down to talk to you." She asked, "Do you want to go over to the house?" I said, "I'll give you a ride." She got on that scooter and sat behind me with her legs sticking out as she was hanging on to me. We sailed the half mile over there! When we got over to the house, instead of parking, I made a circle a couple of times. We enjoyed that.

We talked, and I said, "You've got debts and too much of a burden to handle. The house is half done, and you don't need me as a weight around your neck. You have kids in school, and you're carrying an awful load. I'm not going to stay. I'm going back to Oakley." I told her I'd make out. I'd found jobs working in the filling station, the grocery store and unloading boxcars. We had an argument. She insisted, "You've got to come back and finish high school!" I said, "I can't! I've got to keep going!" She said, "No, you don't!"

I insisted, "Yes, I do!" I told her, "I'll tell you what, I'll go back to Oakley, talk to the principal and see if I can go to school half a day and work for this carpenter the other half and get my diploma." I'd already talked to the carpenter, Mr. Sellers, and he said I could. She said, "If you'll do that, that'll be okay."

I went up to the school in Oakley and talked to the principal. He wouldn't agree to my plan because he said if he let me do that, every kid in the school would want to do the same thing. I told him this was a "have-to" case, but he still wouldn't let me go to school. I didn't tell Mom.

I went back to work on the house for Mr. Sellers, but we were at a lull in the remodeling. I could see the handwriting on the wall, and I was scared. Winter was coming, and it would be so cold. I didn't make enough money to buy food, so I'd use ketchup and hot water to make soup, and I had some crackers. That was my supper. I didn't know if the job with Mr. Sellers would pay enough or last long enough for me to get by, and I was hungry!

I was sitting around thinking about that and wondering what I wanted to do with my life. As I was thinking, I remembered talking with Andy Mendenhall.

When I was in school at Gove, Andy was in the Navy. He would come home on leave and tell me about being in the service. He was very friendly, and I was interested in what he told me. He gave me a Navy cap which I still have. When we were playing basketball, Andy would come over to the high school and play with us. He was like a mentor to me. As he and I talked more, I learned a lot about where he had been. That was where I wanted to be too.

I decided to see if I could get into the Navy. The room I had at that time was on the curve on the south side of Oakley. God was with me because that was right on the route of truckers who came through Oakley on 83 Highway on their way down to Dodge City. This trucker was over there at the filling station, and I went up to him and said, "Can I get a lift?" He asked, "Where you goin'?" I told him, "I think I want to go to Dodge City." He said, "You think?" I said, "Yeah, I'm gonna enlist in the Navy." He said, "Yeah, sure." I got in the truck and rode with him all the way to Dodge.

It was evening when I got there, so I slept on the couch in the hotel lobby. The next morning, I went over to the Navy Recruiting Office. The Recruiting Officer asked, "Can I help you?" I said, "I want to join the Navy." He said, "You don't look big enough to be in the Navy." I told him, "Well, I am." He asked, "How old are you?" I lied and said, "I'm seventeen." I was only sixteen at that time, and I was supposed to have somebody sign the papers for me to enlist. He asked me who was going to sign. I said, "I'm an orphan and don't have anybody to sign." He told me, "Well, go get yourself something to eat and drink and come back after lunch." So, I left with fear and trembling. When I came back, he said, "You're in luck, boy. We found somebody to sign your papers. You go on home. You'll be getting train tickets and meal tickets, and we'll send you a letter letting you know when to be at the depot."

I hitchhiked back to Oakley. I remember riding in a truck, and when I got back and thanked the guy that picked me up, I asked, "Do I owe you anything?" He said, "Well, I could sure use a candy bar." I went into the filling station and bought him one.

When I came back, I went to Mr. Sellers and told him I had enlisted in the Navy. He looked at me and said, "You should have talked to me first because I needed you to work for me all winter."

When I got the letter from the Navy, I was scared to death! I had to give up my room. I packed everything I owned into a big trunk. (It's one that I bought at Penney's.) I asked Arden Numer if I brought my trunk up to his place if he would keep it till someone from Gove could pick it up. He said, "Sure." Mom went up to Oakley later and got it for me.

I had everything ready. It was 4:00 in the morning. I was in the depot in Oakley, standing there looking out that picture window, and there was snow on Main Street. That's when it came to me, "Nobody knows where I am, and nobody gives a _____."

9-24-1946 See letter from Mrs. Clifford Bland with whom Donald Shugart is living at Gove, Kansas, saying Donald wished to go into the Navy and insisted that she sign papers so she could give her consent to his enlistment. Mr. Bland died in August 1945. The recruiting officer planned to be there September 26 and Mrs. Bland asked that we get in touch with Jesse Linder, county attorney at Gove, regarding this matter.

I found from letters in the record that on July 19, 1945 a letter was written to Mr. Hegler asking him to prepare papers transferring guardianship from the League to Mr. Clifford

Bland of Gove, Kansas. This was in reply to a letter from Mr. Bland asking for that guardianship. Since there was nothing further in the record of the correspondence about this matter, I called Mr. Ben Hegler, attorney, and gave him the facts about the case and the recent letter. Mr. Hegler…would talk to the county attorney in Gove about the matter. I told him I would appreciate having a letter from him telling me what plan he made with Mr. Linder about Donald.

11-1-1946 Talked with Mr. Hegler. Letter of Guardianship received on this date from the Probate Judge at Abilene, Kansas. Mr. Hegler, who was visited by the Navy Recruiting Officer, as President of the League, gave his consent for Donald Earl Shugart to join the Navy.[1]

SIXTEEN

THE NAVY — FINDING MY NICHE

I really was so scared! I rode non-stop to Kansas City on a streamliner. I think it was called the "City of St. Louis" which, at that time, went between St. Louis and Cheyenne.[1]

In Kansas City, several of us got off the train, and the Navy put us up in a motel. The next morning there were about fifty of us who had to strip off all our clothes except our shorts, and the doctors examined us. As we went through the line, we didn't know if we were going to be sailors or not. When the day was over, everybody passed except one guy who had heart problems or something.

We had to take a test to get into the service, and I was afraid I might fail. God was with me again, and I was accepted into the Navy. When we passed everything, we each held up our right hand and swore to support the United States Constitution and the United States military with our lives.

While we were there in Kansas City, we were interviewed to see what we could do and what we already knew. They asked us what we did when we were growing up. Some of the guys did quite a lot of extra work, and some of them just went to high school. I told them I had worked in a grocery store, was a filling station attendant, farm hand, had unloaded boxcars and had done a little carpentry work helping rehab a house.

The man interviewing me asked, "What do you want to do?" I said, "I want to be an aviation mechanic and work on airplanes." He said, "Sorry, we don't need any more mechanics. We have a lot of them left over from World War II." I asked him, "What have you got?" That's when he said to me, "Well, there are two things. Number one is you live here in Kansas City and go to school every day. You work with some company that has cards, and they punch holes in them." I said, "That doesn't sound very interesting." He said, "Well, they need guys to work on those." I thought I'd gotten myself stuck in that. I asked again what it was. He told me, "All I know is that it has big letters that say IBM." I asked him what that meant. He said, "I don't know." I told him I didn't want that.

He said, "The second position I have is AETM (Aviation Electronics Technician Mate). I asked, "What's that one?" He told me, "You're not supposed to talk about it. It's top secret, and it has to do with surveillance." I didn't know what that was. He explained that it was to help check out places where there could be people that are dangerous to America. I asked him what I would do. He said, "Well, you're supposed to learn how to fix this equipment." I asked, "What does the equipment do?" He told me he didn't know, but it had to do with electronics and had radios in it. I perked up a little. He said, "The school is over a year long, and it's in Corpus Christi." I asked him, "Where's Corpus Christi?"

He told me it was in Texas, and I agreed to go there.

The next day, we were given our papers and one set of clothes — drawers, pants and a shirt. We were getting ready to be loaded up and taken down to the depot in Kansas City heading for San Diego. We were all ready to go, and the officer in charge wanted somebody to carry the packets of records for every man who was getting on the train. He said, "Bland, you carry these to San Diego, but you'll be in big trouble if you lose them!" I had to carry those in my suitcase. We got there and boarded the train.

Some of those guys were cocky. They wanted to get off and buy some whiskey when we'd stop at a town to take on coal or water. When they'd hear the whistle, they'd come running like a bunch of jackrabbits and jump back on that old coal-burner train. I had to make sure everyone was accounted for.

There were a lot of us from Kansas. When we got off the train in San Diego, it was 70 degrees, a big difference from when I left Oakley only a few days before when it was "spittin' snow."

They had buses waiting for us and took us out to the Naval Training Center at Point Loma. That's where we spent the next four months in boot camp learning what we were going to do while we were in the service. That was the start of my Navy career.

The first thing the Master Chief told all of us was, "You're going to sit down and write a letter to your family and tell them where you are." They even had stationery, so I couldn't cop out on that. I wrote to Mom and told her I was in San Diego in the Navy and thanked her for taking care of me and giving me a home for the time I had been with them and that I appreciated it very much.

There were very few of us who went down to Corpus Christi to the Naval Air Technical Training Center at Ward Island (NATTC).[2] We rode a coal-burner train to Corpus Christi then went on to the training school at Ward Island south of there. There were barracks, an administration building, instructional buildings, mess halls, the gym and a large swimming pool used for training. You couldn't get into the Technical Compound restricted area unless you had a pass. When we went ashore, we had to take a very small boat to get over to land.

Something else that interested me was that there were four or five air strips nearby at the Naval Air Station.

I found out that the Russians weren't supposed to know that the school at Corpus Christi on Ward Island was there. What we did was highly classified, so our training was located on that island [actually a peninsula].

In the school, we had to take tests, and they kept track of our GPA. Many of the guys failed. The schooling started out with mathematics all the way up through algebra, geometry and trigonometry. I had studied algebra and geometry in high school at Gove, so that wasn't so hard, but trigonometry was. I stumbled on the course that covered the powers of ten. I was dumbfounded. It took me two shots at it, but I finally got it. From then on, I just worked my way through the classes. They said we needed all of that schooling so we could read the dials and everything on the electronic equipment to make the planes work right.

We were there to learn electronics, radar, sonar and underwater torpedoes among other things. We also learned to swim for survival. We had to be able to swim underwater the length of the pool. They trained us that if we ever had to jump into water with burning fuel on top, to swim with our palms facing outward so that our faces would be protected by our hands as the water was scooped away from us. When we were first doing training drills, I thought that was the stupidest thing in the world. Later I realized this was very valuable training for saving our lives.

They taught us how this secret operation for which we were being trained would work. They never told us what it was. When we graduated from NATTC, we had a big celebration, and those of us who passed were sent back to San Diego. We thought we were going overseas.

SEVENTEEN
BACK TO SAN DIEGO

When we got out of the training center, there were guys who were sweeping the streets because the new planes that we were going to fly in hadn't been built yet and there wasn't much for us to do. Because I knew how to type, they sent me across the water to North Island in a little boat that we called a "nickel snatcher." The Lieutenant Commander put me to work as his private secretary. There were four of us in the office which was adjacent to his. It was there that they taught me how to run a spread sheet and use the powers of ten and other things having to do with mathematics.

The Lieutenant Commander had me do everything for him. He had the nicest car, which I would drive down to Point Loma to fill up with gas.

I was assigned a scooter with a side car on it. Part of my job at the time was to ride over to the chow hall and check on whether the cooks were getting the supplies they needed. As they were feeding everyone, I had to go through the galley and talk to the cooks.

One day, five sailors from Grainfield, Jimmy Grecian, Rudy Dinkel, Francis Cox, Buzzy Lanham (if I remember their names correctly) and one other guy, saw me on that scooter. Rudy Dinkel called out to me, "Hey, Bland!" I had known them all before I joined the Navy, and it was "old home week" as we talked right there in front of the chow hall.

When I was finished, I'd get back on my scooter, go across the base to my office on the north side, then make my report and give it to the Lieutenant Commander. I told him I wanted to get back into the Air Navy instead of being a yeoman. He wanted me to stay on with him and said, "You're doing a good job," but I explained to him, "I want to go to sea."

Sometime after that, I got a call saying I had been transferred to the Naval Air Station North Island, which was across from the training center, where all the big ships (aircraft carriers, battleships, destroyers and others that were in the Pacific fleet) come into the DES Base. That's where those ships coming in from the Pacific were repaired. I got over there where they were going to assign me to a plane crew, but the planes still weren't built yet, so I was assigned as an SP (shore patrol) for the Naval Air Station at San Diego.

I spent several months policing things that went on at the base. We were there to make sure no unauthorized people entered day or night. There were some interesting stories from that time, which I won't tell here. We did that for a while until they finally got the planes built. Of course, we didn't know much about the planes at the time, nor did we know where they were. Everything was kept secret.

One of my favorite things to do for entertainment while I was on North Island was to go hear the big bands that played in large auditoriums around San Diego. I would take enough money to buy a Pepsi to sip on while I sat listening to that beautiful music. They played clear through the evening, and I loved it.

One time that sticks in my memory was when I was going onshore, and one of the other sailors wanted to go with me. So we put on our dress blues, and away we went. The big band was there playing all their wonderful music.

As I was listening to the band play "Stormy Weather," I heard somebody crying. I couldn't figure out who it was. I turned around, and realized it was my friend bawling like a baby. I asked him what was wrong. He said, "I want to go home!" He had just been in the Navy for a short time and decided he didn't like it. I said, "Well, buddy, you've got a problem. You've got to serve your time." That didn't help. He just kept on sobbing. I said, "Don't do that because I want to listen to the music." He finally shut up so we could hear.

We went back to the barracks, and about a week or so later I was ready to go again. He said, "Where are you going?" I told him, "I'm going onshore." He wanted to go along, but I wouldn't let him because I didn't want him to interrupt the music again.

One of the singers I got to hear was Bing Crosby. His song, "I'll Be Home for Christmas," was popular at that time. I spent several Christmases away from home while

I was in the Navy, and that became my theme song during the holidays. "I'll be home for Christmas — if only in my dreams."

———————

During that time, I got a letter which began something like, "Dear Don, My name is Maryetta, and I am your sister." She told me about each of my siblings. She said that our birth order is: Maryetta, Marion, Bob, Dorothy, Hershel, me and Herbie.

She said that my brother, Marion, was in the Air Force in California, and he would like to see me. She gave me his mother-in-law's house number in Orange County. I got the telephone book and very cautiously called him and told him who I was. He said, "Well, it's been a long time." I said, "Yeah!" He was up in the Mojave Desert where they were testing military airplanes. He and his family lived in a military house trailer there. He had previously been in the Navy, but when his time was up, he was discharged and immediately joined the Air Force.

We arranged to meet sometime later at his mother-in-law's house. I took the address and went up there. There he was with his wife, Lila, two sons, "Buddy" (Preston) and "Mo" (Merle) and his mother-in-law all standing on the porch. They came over to greet me, and we spent the whole weekend talking and talking about what had happened during the years we had lost. We had a good time together.

He told me that he was at Pearl Harbor when the Japanese attacked. He was sleeping on his ship when the attack began. He woke up when the ship began listing and felt himself turning over. He ran as fast as he could and jumped over the side of the ship. There was fire everywhere! He was picked up by a Jon boat. Those boats were sweeping Pearl Harbor picking up the wounded and drowning who were then taken to the hospital. They also picked up many bodies of men who had been killed in the attack.

Marion's original ship was downed by the Japanese. When he lost his ship, he was reassigned to another one, the USS Pennsylvania, which was chasing the Japanese across the Pacific from island to island. He was later assigned to the USS La Salle.

He was made a pilot (boatswain mate) of a Higgins Boat,[1] named after A. J. Higgins. They made landings on every island, dumping Marines off and then backing up. Some of the islands were: Kwajalein, Wake Island, Midway, Guadalcanal and Iwo Jima.

The way the Higgins boats were used was that there was a mother ship out in the bay, and the Higgins boats would come along side. The Marines would come down the rope ladder, and when the count got high enough, they wouldn't let any more aboard. They would circle out there with eight to ten Higgins boats, and then they would all take off for the beach. There was safety in numbers because with more boats out there, fewer men would die. They would come in wide open; the sand would stop them; and they'd drop the front gate. The Marines would be unloaded out of the Higgins boats, and it was up to them to take the island. They took most of the islands in the South Pacific. The area from Pearl Harbor and on south was the job of the Marines and the Navy. The Navy had the boats, and the Marines did most of the fighting although the Navy was also armed and ready to fight, which they did.

They were getting ready to go to Okinawa, and after being shot at numerous times, Marion got scared. He went to the chaplain on the ship and said, "I've made five or six landings, and I think my time's up." The chaplain talked to him. Marion said, "I think I've got a brother who is supposed to be somewhere in Kansas, and I'd like to know where he's at before I die. They said he died, but I don't think he did." The chaplain took all the information and said, "Okay, I'll see what I can do for you."

Marion said that sometime after that, they were waiting to load up and were coming down the rope ladder to get into the boat. The chaplain hollered at him over the radio, "Marion, come up here!" The military and God Himself got information through to the chaplain telling Marion that I was alive and well, living somewhere in west Kansas, and they even gave him my grades in high school. The chaplain said, "He's all right." Marion asked, "Well, where is he?" The chaplain said, "I can't tell you. The Red Cross sealed a pact with the Kansas Children's Home and Service League that they can't tell anyone where he is."

As I was listening to Marion talk about that, I thought, "It's a lie. Nobody cares about me like that." I didn't believe him, but I pretended I did. Many years later when I was able to get my file from the Kansas Children's Home and Service League, there's a copy of the letter that the Red Cross wrote asking for information about his brother. I had to realize that Marion wasn't bluffing me and was telling the truth. Even though I thought "Nobody does that," they really do! Marion was the first one of my natural siblings I got to meet after being separated from them for so many years.

———————

THE AMERICAN RED CROSS
SHAWNEE COUNTY CHAPTER
TOPEKA, KANSAS

February 12, 1945

Kansas Children's Home And Service League
918 Kansas Avenue
Topeka, Kansas

RE: SHUGART, Marion Walter SF 2/c
Shugart, Donald (Address Unknown)
Attention: Mr. Albert Stoneman:

Dear Sirs:

We recently received a request from the Chaplin [sic] *of the U.S.S. La Salle asking that we contact your agency to obtain information regarding Donald Shugart, brother of Marion Shugart who is in the United States Navy.*

It is our understanding that in 1931 Marion Walter Shugart and his brother, Donald Shugart were placed under the jurisdiction of the Kansas Children's Home and Service League by Judge Scott of Dickerson [sic] *County. An aunt took three of them, but the youngest child of the four, Donald had already been adopted. It is our understanding that at that time, the father and mother, Mr. & Mrs. Walter M. Shugart had separated. Shortly before this, the mother was in the hospital and when she was released from there, the sailor states that his mother tried to find her son, Donald, but without success.*

If it is possible for your agency to release any information to our office regarding this particular case, we will be greatly appreciative of this service as the sailor is very desirous of locating his brother. An answer at your earliest convenience will be greatly appreciated.

Very truly yours,
(Mrs.) Dora A. Payne
Executive Secretary

(Miss) Florence Walker
Home Service Worker

FW/pm²

EIGHTEEN

ON LEAVE — SHE SAID "YES!"

Berniece and her mother paid her way to attend Colorado Women's College after she graduated from high school in Oakley in 1947. I came home on leave, stopped in Denver and went to the college to see her. We went out on a date. Later she rode the bus back to Oakley with me; then I went down to Gove to stay with Mom and the family.

I had a date with Berniece, and believe it or not, Mom let me use her car. I went to Oakley to pick up Berniece. She had a cousin who had invited us down for supper at their house in Scott City. The four of us sat around and talked, and then it was time for me to get her back to Oakley.

There used to be a little town between Scott City and Oakley called Elkader. There wasn't much there, maybe just a store. Well, we were driving north, riding along talking, and I said to her casually, "Would you marry me, Berniece?" I had asked that before, and nothing had happened. All at once, she said, "Yes, I would." I just about put Mom's car in the ditch! I stopped the car right there at that little town, and we had a smooch before I took her back to Oakley.

The next day, she had to go back to Denver, and I had

to go back to the Navy. I packed my clothes at Mom's place and said my goodbyes to the family. Somebody took me to Oakley. Berniece and I rendezvoused there and then got on a bus to head back.

We took a bus down to a jeweler in Denver, and I bought her a diamond ring with some money I had laid back from the Navy. You have a hard time seeing it because it's so danged small, but to her it was big.

In her diary, Berniece wrote, "My dad says not to marry Don because I can do a lot better, but I told him that I'm going to marry him."

We said our goodbyes at Colorado Women's College. The song lyrics, "I'll see you in my dreams, hold you in my dreams," played over and over in my mind. I caught a bus or train (usually the Greyhound Bus) and rode back to San Diego. Life was altogether different after Berniece said she would marry me. I wrote her a letter every night, and she wrote me one every day too. I still have some of them.

One Saturday back in San Diego after being able to go ashore, I went out to see the world. I went up to a tattoo stand. The guy put a stencil on my arm, sprayed it a little, took the stencil off and then started filling it in with ink. It's special to me. If you look at it closely, you'll see there's a blank spot at an angle. There is an arrow going through it. That's where Berniece's name goes, but I never did have it put in.

NINETEEN
WHIDBEY ISLAND

My next assignment was at Whidbey Island, Washington. I was stationed at Ault Field, which is clear out on the peninsula in the "toolies" of Washington where they kept all the top-secret stuff. We rode a bus from San Diego through San Francisco to Seattle. We couldn't get to Ault Field because it was snowed in, so we had to get a motel for the night. The next day, they brought in a truck to pick us up and take us to Whidbey Island. You can't even get a ride out of that place to go on liberties. We had to figure out how to get to shore. It was several miles to the nearest town.

When I got to Whidbey, I held the rank of Petty Officer Third Class — SK3 (Storekeeper Third Class) and was working as a Supply Officer. They were finding a place for us while we continued to wait for the planes to be built. I wasn't going to work in the galley. A lot of the guys signed up for Seabees, which was "a wheelbarrow and three shovels." I didn't want that. The guy argued with me. He said, "Well, you know how to drive a tractor, don't you?" I joked, "Not anymore."

They finally got the planes finished. We weren't supposed to take pictures of them, but I took one anyway. We couldn't talk about the planes either. In fact, we couldn't tell anybody that we were electronic technicians. My flight jacket had an insignia on it that did not represent what I was.

Our job was to fly the Aleutian Chain and down to Sand Point Naval Air Station north of Seattle. When World War II was over, many of the fighter pilots were burned out and were going home. They didn't want any more of it, nor did they ever want to see another fighter or bomber! Because of that, they didn't have enough pilots for all these new two-engine bombers, the Lockheed P-2 Neptune (P2V's).[1]

In those days between World War II and the Korean War, Congress offered what they called "flight skins" to Petty Officers Second and Third-Class who wanted to train to become pilots. We'd just go down to the office and request to get on the flight list. I did that and was getting an extra $50 a month for flying four hours a day at second seat. I was working on getting my pilot's license. We would fly up over the Aleutian Chain and down to Seattle then back to Whidbey Island. I wrote down my hours. I have them in my book. I flew to Sand Point and up the Aleutian Chain a lot.

I was learning to fly one of those planes, second seat. The pilot would say, "Okay, Bland, take over." We had a heading of where we were going. We'd go north of Seattle to the Naval Air Station (NAS) Seattle at Sand Point.[2]

We'd land there and do touch-and-gos. You'd come in for a landing and set the wheels on the ground, let it go about 20 feet, then give the power to it, pull it back and fly off, make a big circle, then come back and bring it in, put the tires on the blacktop, go a little way, hit the throttle and go again. We'd count them, and we got so much time on each one. If we did fifty touch-and-gos, that counted toward getting our license. I was well into getting mine.

This program was during the Cold War with Russia, even though we didn't know about a "Cold War" at the time. When the equipment finally came, we had to put it in the airplanes, hook it up and get it ready.

In those times before the Korean War started, the big problem was Russian submarines. The Pacific Northwest was full of them. The Russians owned submarine pens at Nome, Alaska. Our equipment was used to search out the North Pacific, in the Aleutians, where the Russian subs were hiding. We could search for them from the air. The planes had been designed so that when we'd get down to 1,000 feet or so, we'd lower a periscope, sit there at the gauges, and the electronic equipment would pick up any sub in the area for miles around. I know it works because I've done it.

When we were flying around 3,000 feet, we could see the whole thing. We would count the sub pens. From the air, they looked like about twelve or fourteen trench silos put together side by side. Submarines from Russia were stationed there, and they would come in at night into those sub pens. We'd fly over them the next day and count them. When we'd find, for instance, that eight and nine subs were gone, we'd fly out of there over the Aleutian Chain and go get them.

We had an idea of which way they would go. Some of them would go toward Seattle and some would go toward

Japan. We'd find them from the air with radar gear and radio signals. As we'd fly over, we could tell by the way the water was being broken that there was a sub down there.

From the plane, we'd drop a radio-controlled sonar device inside a red tile. When it hit the water, it would open up. The device would come out of it; the radio would float; and we could talk to that sonobuoy. It would be picked up later by a tugboat. Everything was in there. There were two radios (one to find them and one to operate a directional finder) and a float.

We could zero in on them and find where the subs were. We could be quite a distance away because we were in the air. They were in the water, and they couldn't move very fast. We could know where to go to hit them. When we would find a sub, at first, we didn't do much, but then it got so that we would drop a signal right on top of their sub so they would know that they'd been hit, and they would back off.

When we found them, the Russians were notified that we'd found one of their subs, and the sub operator would get chastised when he got back to Russia. Our mission was surveillance and reporting.

In that short time, I learned a lot. I think there were eight or nine guys in the plane. Everyone had a desk, an earphone and everything it took to run the equipment. When we got ready to take off from Whidbey Island, the captain on the plane (who was not part of our organization) would have to tell us what we were up against. He'd say, "Okay, men, your weather gear, you got it with you?" He would go through all of this like he did a million times before. We'd say, "Yeah." Inside a big case, we'd find wolf-skin coats, boots, gloves, and May West life vests. We could wear the coats, boots and gloves in the plane to keep our hands from freezing. We'd tell him, "We already know all that." He'd remind us, "It's the Navy rules to make sure you have your equipment with you. I've got to tell you, but I guess you don't need to know because if you jump out of this plane, you're only going to last seven minutes cause the water's so cold." We'd think, "Gee thanks, chief!" Then we would quit joking and get serious. There were two World War II rifles strapped to the ceiling for our use if we were shot down or had an accident and had to ditch.

They reminded us of our training to never to put our hands together with palms facing in when we jumped into the water but to jump in with our palms facing out to protect our faces if there was burning diesel fuel on top of the water.

We would fly up and down the West Coast, the Aleutian Chain and almost to the North Pole, then turn around and come back through Nome, Alaska, and on over to China and back. I've flown over lots of land in different places but never put my feet on the ground there. We'd come back and land. We had so many hours that we had to fly to find submarines. I called it hide and seek. When we landed out on the Aleutian Chain, which we did four times every two weeks, we'd fly out there, land, survey and then come back from Kodiak.

It was foggy some of the time. Because the fog would be 10–20 feet deep, we couldn't see the runway. Our pilots got good enough that they would fly a few feet off the water and when they would come to where the gravel started, they would give 'er the gun, pull the plane up and set it down without even seeing the runway much ahead of time. Of course, the prop would kick the fog out of the way so then we could see where to land.

When the Korean War broke out, they recalled those World War II pilots who had stayed in the reserves, and said, "Come on back, boys, you're going to Korea." They were retraining those pilots, so they were ready to go. That ended the "flight skins" and the extra $50 a month for us to become pilots because those guys were officers and had preference over us. It was just one of those things that happened.

If the Korean War hadn't started, I'd have been an AP1 (Aviation Pilot First Class). I got in enough flying hours to get my second seat pilot's license, but I was trying to get my AP1 pilot's license. There were a few of the guys who made AP1 while they were there. When one of them became a certified pilot, they put his name on his airplane and AP1 on the tail.

I had three stripes but without the "V." I think I would have had to go up two steps to get to be AP1. I don't know how much longer, maybe a year, and I would have had my military combat pilot's license. I wanted to do that so bad, so I was going to stay in, but that didn't work out.

Another reason they cut us off was because we couldn't get enough gasoline. The refineries weren't producing it fast enough, so, of course, the ones going to Korea had priority. I could not figure that out. When World War II was going on, everybody had extra. If they wanted five trucks, they got ten of them. There was excess everywhere. At the time of the invasion of France on D-Day, June 6, 1944, the military had so much equipment. There were pictures of many acres covered with trucks and tanks that they had built, lined up, and taken over to England and had them ready for the invasion. Those were loaded onto barges and hauled into France almost overnight.

RIGHT: Donald Shugart at Children's Home in Topeka, Kansas.

LEFT: Cora Shugart with Donald.

RIGHT: Shugart brothers — Hershel, Bob, Marion and Donald (on tricycle) at Children's Home in Topeka, Kansas.

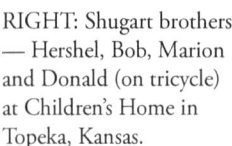

LEFT: Donald's biological parents, Cora and Walter Shugart at their home in Dillon, Kansas.

BELOW: Cast iron toy truck. Donald's only keepsake from his childhood before western Kansas.

BELOW: Shugart family — Dorothy, Bob, Hershel, Cora, Marion, Herbert, Walter, Maryetta at their home in Dillon, Kansas. Donald was already in western Kansas.

Early Years

At the age of thirteen I was told that I did not have a name and did not belong in the home where I was living.

Remembrances are few of my early life. I was born into a large family whose father was unaccountable and an alcoholic, a mother who could not cope with her world.

The dim memory I have in being in the Kansas Children's home at the age 2½. I later learned from my siblings had been made a ward of the court and taken out of the home. I remember playing on a shinning wood floor with a larger person protecting my toys from other kids but he did not have a face.

Two months after my third birthday I was placed on a train with a man who took me to western Kansas. It was a cold and windy Nov night when we step off on the train in Grainfield. I stood by the big steam engine as the two men talked in the dim light of the depot. I was lonely and scared and did not understand what was happening. The man from the Kansas Children Home told me to go with the man he was talking to who later I learned was Amos Bland.

Amos was a man who was barely a itinerant farmer who at the time was contracted carrying the mail. He and his wife, Leita, had a daughter Maxine. My presence there I learned later was for the cause of not having to go through the process of child birth. Not having to suffer pain. I was there to have, not to hold as there was no love shown in the family.

ABOVE: Written by Don.

RIGHT: Don shortly after arriving at Amos and Leita Bland's home in Grainfield, Kansas.

ABOVE: Amos, Don, Maxine, Leita.

RIGHT: Maxine, Amos and Don.

BELOW: Maxine (5) and Don (3),
September 1933.

ABOVE: James S. Bland and sons — Forest, Jean, Cliff, Ross, James S., Amos.

LEFT: Don on Joe Losey's horse "Cupid" — July 1938.

BELOW ON LEFT: James S. Bland and sons with their horses and mules.

BELOW: Cliff Bland (front) Roman riding in a race.

ABOVE LEFT: Don with one of his bummer lambs from Joe Losey.

ABOVE RIGHT: Don with Amos' 1941 Ford.

LEFT: Grade school class in Gove — Don third from left in front.

RIGHT: Don in the Navy hat from Andy Mendenhall. The horse was given to him by Don Tustin.

ABOVE: Shocking feed at Leita's.

BELOW: Bicycle Don bought from Isleys with money
he earned by selling bummer lambs.

My life, from the time I can remember
was built on two words. They were
Duty and Honer! It was a duty of everyone
to preform according to an established
set of rules. No Love was involved
it was a matter of fact. Go outside of
the expected rules and be punished. The
form being anything between physical, verbal
and shunned. The Honor was really for
Public Opinion - living in a small comunity.
Honer realy ment, don't cause any embarrasment

Love:
Love was never a part of my life from the
earliest time I remember, There was a great vacume
inside which was never filled. I could feel it,
a sence of aloneness, longing to be filled. In
the years before becoming a teenager, The
song, "Somewhere over the Rainbow, was poplar
and it exposed my heart desire. My desire
for music was born in those years. It
seemed like a way to express the emotions

LiFe:
I remember even at the age of three, That
something was missing, although not able to
remember my early childhood. there were glimpses
or flashes of early youth, Being

ABOVE: Duty and Honor — written by Don.

large room with a lot of kids. A person beside me protecting me. No face, just a person. Years later, I learned he was an older sibling.

As life began with the Blodford there was someone to play with. "Mopine" I was shown off, to all the clan the months. The Blnds were a very clanish people and when they came together blood sealed the unity, not love! I was to learn early that, I was a spectator in the family. There were the age old family stories, the ills they liked, the heart aches, and a mircel of other accomplishments. Here again Duty and Honor prevailed. We moved several times before I was a teenager. The Blnds never saw fit to adopt me, and so Every 3 to six months a Case worker, would be around to check on my Physical well being. Being in a small comunity, it was well known that I was an orphan. When the name calling and laughter from other kids came it hurt and when looking for comfort, none came. Duty and Honor did.

ABOVE: Duty and Honor.

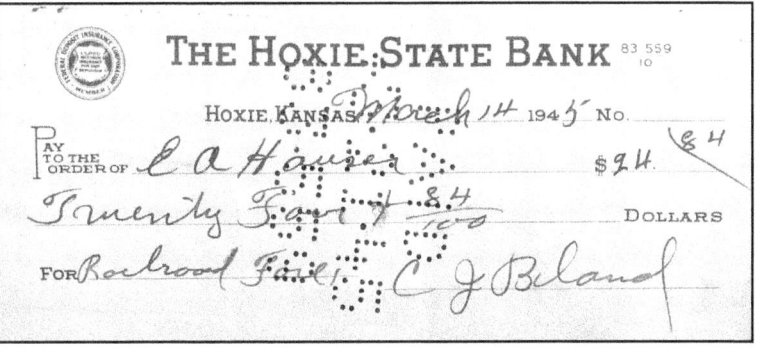

ABOVE LEFT: Marie, Don and Maxine at Leita's.

ABOVE RIGHT: Back — Claude and Olive Simmons, Don. Front — Maxine, cousins Donna and Janet Tustin.

LEFT: Don at Leita's shortly before being sent away.

BELOW: Check for train tickets to Topeka to get Don. *Courtesy Karen Bland.*

THE HOXIE STATE BANK

83 559
10

HOXIE, KANSAS *March 14* 1945 No.

PAY TO THE ORDER OF *C A Hauser* $24.84

Twenty Four + 84/100 DOLLARS

FOR *Railroad Fare* *C J Bland*

TOP: Gove High School Basketball team with coach Oren Daniels —
the day before Don was sent away — March 2, 1945.

ABOVE LEFT: Berniece and Don — high school sweethearts.

ABOVE RIGHT: Don's "Dad" —
Sheriff Cliff Bland in his office at Gove, Kansas.

LEFT: Don's "Mom" — Ethel Bland — circa 1970s.

BELOW: Note to Ethel from Don.

Mothers Day 1980

Dear Mom
    As I travel down lifes road and look back at my life I thank God for your love and care for me when I needed you.
    In my search for the past I find, still, you are and always be my Mom. I love you

Donald E Bland

LEFT: Don in the Navy
at age seventeen.

BELOW: SPs (Shore Patrol)
at North Island, San Diego.
Don second from left in front.

LEFT: Ward Island —
Corpus Christi, Texas.

ABOVE: Supply office at Whidbey.

LEFT: Don writing a letter
back home.

RIGHT: Don and his Lieutenant Commander at Kodiak, Alaska.

BELOW: Berniece and Don at Colorado Women's College.

BELOW: Grumman F6F Hellcat (F6) — a propeller from one of these hit Don on the head.

ABOVE: Fuel truck Don
drove at Kodiak.

ABOVE: Lockheed P-2 Neptune
(P2V) — the aircraft Don flew
at Whidbey Island.

LEFT: Marion Shugart (with wife, Lila)
and Don meeting for the first time
as adults — Orange County, California.

RIGHT: Don's "beautiful blonde" as a student at Colorado Women's College.

BELOW: Don and Berniece on their wedding day — February 20, 1951.

RIGHT: Attendants, Carolyn Tustin and Wayne Bland, with the newlyweds.

ABOVE: Berniece's parents,
Harlan and Lorane Tustin.

RIGHT: Don's bride at Whidbey Island
where they spent many memorable evenings
down by the water.

LEFT: Don's biological siblings —
Don, Maryetta, Bob, Dorothy and
Hershel at Ethel Bland's farm,
Gove, Kansas. The first time they saw
each other in almost two decades.

ABOVE: Back — Bonnie Shugart, Maryetta
Dashnow, Berniece Bland, Dorothy Strand.
Middle — Hershel Shugart, Bob Shugart,
Don Bland. Front — Allanna Dashnow,
Dianna Dashnow, Connie Strand —
November 1951.

BELOW: Ethel Bland family — Wayne, Elinor,
Don, Marie, Kenneth, Clifford Jr., Ethel.

ABOVE: Berniece
and Donnie (nine
months old) at the
farm at Levant.

BELOW: Robbie
(thirteen months old)
at the farm.

ABOVE: Back — Linda and Gail Beesley.
Middle — Don, Clifford, Dora, Berniece, Elinor,
Mae, Ethel. Front — Marie and Marvin Beesley,
Wayne, Boyd, Kenneth.

LEFT: Jody and Don
cooling off in the stock
tank at the farm.

RIGHT: Harry Barnett, preacher at
Winona Methodist Church.

BELOW: Jesus Christ and His bummer lamb.

RIGHT: Jody, Rob, and Donnie at the
family home in Lakewood, Colorado.

BELOW: Don's first airplane —
172 Cessna.

ABOVE: Don's second airplane — 182 Cessna.

New Southwest Subdivision

A new housing development has opened in southwest Denver. Chuck Kline of Spartan Homes is showing four new models at 2005 S. Cape Way in Green Gables. The homes are in the $16,000 to $18,000 price class and include Lennox forced air furnaces and General Electric kitchens. Styles range from ranch type to tri-level and even a four-level

LEFT: Chuck Kline who helped Don get started in Denver.

RIGHT: The generator Don wired in Lima, Peru.

ABOVE: Men at the Lima House.

BELOW: Herbie, Don, Hershel, Dorothy, Bob at a park in Wichita.

ABOVE: Don's family — Berniece, Donnie, Jody, Don and Rob.

BELOW LEFT: Wiring for Wycliffe.

BELOW RIGHT: Two Dons building the shop and
house in rural McPherson.

ABOVE: Ninetieth birthday party. Rob, Don, Donnie and Jody.

RIGHT: In front of the house Don built for Berniece northwest of McPherson, Kansas.

ABOVE LEFT: Don with Merrill Eisenhower Atwater —
great-grandson of President Eisenhower.

ABOVE RIGHT: Don at Dwight D. Eisenhower
Presidential Library & Museum.

ABOVE: Don with Barbara Zimmerman revisiting
the church where they were saved in September 1962.

TWENTY
CHUCK AND DON KLINE

One of the World War II pilots was my cousin, Chuck Kline, though I didn't know him well at that time. Years later he told me his story. He and his squadron had been waiting for the new airplanes, the Corsairs,[1] to come into the Marine Station at Miramar, San Diego, California.

Chuck told me that Charles Lindbergh flew one of the new Corsairs into California. "He [Charles Lindbergh] demonstrated how United States Marine Corps Aviation pilots could take off safely with a bomb load double the Vought F4U Corsair fighter-bomber's rated capacity."[2]

Chuck was flying a Corsair and was on a Navy transport ship, but it wasn't one of the big ones. It was an escort carrier called a "Jeep Carrier." It had a deck that the planes could take off from, but it wasn't long enough to land on. Instead, the pilots would land on a Japanese island.

They had to be trained to fly the Corsairs because this new plane flew pretty rough. It's interesting because the Corsair was designed with gull wings which made the plane act like a scoop when it hit the water causing a water draft, and it would be sucked right down. There were no ejector seats in those days. The pilots were instructed that if they got shot down, they were to open the canopy as soon as they could, bail over the side and get away from the plane as fast as possible. If the pilot didn't get out and away from the plane, they would go down with it and drown.

When Chuck was finished with active duty, he told me, "I've decided I'm gonna get out of the Reserves. I don't like this anymore!" He put in to get out and they let him.

—————————

Chuck's brother, Don Kline, and I were at Whidbey Island at the same time. He wasn't a pilot but was one of the crewmen on a P2V. He was in electronics like I was. I knew his plane. Some of those P2V observation planes had all the electronics taken out so bomb bays could be put in. (That's a rack that stands upright and has about four rows of bombs in it.) When they flew over a target, they'd trip it and drop the bombs.

Our plane didn't have bombs because we were in reconnaissance, finding subs and reporting their location but not shooting them. The government knew where the subs were because we gave them all the information.

Don went over to Korea with a squadron of other P2V's. They were told to fly low so they could kill more North Koreans. Well, those planes were made of aluminum, and about half of the squadron got shot down. Each plane had seven or eight guys in it. Those men died as they went down into the waters of the Sea of Japan. Don was in one of the planes that limped back into Whidbey Island. I went out there as fast as I could because I saw his plane's number. I was so glad to see him! Needless to say, he was shaken up! So was I!

TWENTY ONE
KODIAK

After Whidbey Island I was sent to Kodiak, Alaska, because my time in the service had been extended for one year due to the start of the Korean War. I had to go back to serving in the Supply Office and in the Disbursing Office.

We had gas trucks just like the old trucks back home that would haul gasoline to the farms. They would hold about 8,000 gallons of fuel. Sometimes when we had duty, we had to take them up on the hill where the gas tanks were buried and fill them up. We'd put the gas hose into the tank and turn on the electricity to the pump.

It was cold up there. No one wants to freeze to death standing out there watching the truck, so we'd go into the little shack, sit down in there and time it. To fill that second tank, we'd go back out a little before the time was up so we wouldn't have any problems.

One weekend I took one of the trucks up to fill it as usual. We had been told that the baffles were cut out of the tanks on this truck, so we could fill the whole truck from two lids. (There were usually about four or five lids). I thought, "This is going to be a snap," so I started the pump, went inside to watch the time. While I was waiting, I picked up one of the comic books that was in the shack, started reading it and pretty soon I smelled something.

That gasoline was 145 octane airplane gas, and it was a purple color. I went outside, and the gas was running down the hill in the snow right beside the mess hall where the guys were eating. I thought, "Oh no, I've had it," so I called the fire department, and they came up there and laid foam all up and down that hill!

I had a good skipper, a Lieutenant Commander. Of course, I had done a lot of things for him. He asked, "What happened?" I said, "You don't want to know! I thought the baffles were cut out of the tanks, and I wasn't going to stand out there in the cold and freeze." (I didn't tell him I was reading a funny book.) He said, "I don't blame you." I told him I knew they told us that we were supposed to stay there and watch that meter, but it was really cold in Alaska, sometimes 40 degrees below zero. He said, "Don't worry about it, Bland."

So we had a "Captain's Mast."* The officer in charge said, "What's this case about?" My Lieutenant Commander was speaking for me and said, "We're here about the gas trucks that we have down here to fill up these bombers. Public Service was supposed to cut all the baffles out of them so we could get more gas in them to fly these planes to Japan. We sent orders down to have them cut them out." They've got to have enough gas in them to get over the Aleutian Chain and on to Japan. That's quite a ways.

* A hearing where the commanding officer inquires into the facts concerning offenses.

He put on one of the grandest shows I'd ever seen in my life. I was just saying, "Man, go!" When he got done, the officer in charge said, "Well, I think the fault here lies with Public Service, not with the driver." He told the Lieutenant Commander, "You get a hold of Public Service to get those baffles out of there. We don't need to be wasting gas like that." We got done and were dismissed. I walked out of there and was I ever relieved! My Lieutenant Commander came over to me and said, "See, got you off, didn't I?" I was very thankful for him!

A Lieutenant who stood watch with me in the Disbursing Office told me that he had been on the Bataan death march. The guys (American and Filipino POWs) that were left in the Philippines had to walk sixty-five miles from the southern end of the Bataan Peninsula to San Fernando. Many died along the way. What an awful story that was! He told me lots of stories, some good and some bad.

He tried to teach me a Japanese game called Mahjong which he had learned while he was a prisoner of war. I never did quite get it.

The Imperial Japanese Army who was in power at the time made him and some of the other prisoners assemble Japanese rifles as the guards stood watch. The men would balk when the time came to put in the firing pins. They'd get permission to go to the slit trench (latrine). At the right moment when no one was watching, they'd drop the firing pins into the trench. Those pins were gone forever. If they had been caught, they would have been shot!

One day while there at Kodiak, something happened to me when a guy needed help putting the prop on a plane. I was sent to help him. He was on one side of the plane, and I was on the other. He turned the prop by hand, and it hit me on the head. It knocked me out, and I was taken to sick bay. I don't remember how long I was there, but I still have the scar from that incident.

TWENTY TWO
MARRIED THE LOVE OF MY LIFE

It was at this time while I was at Kodiak that Berniece and I planned to get married. We had picked a date in February, and everything was all set. Berniece did all the wedding preparation and had invited the guests. As the day approached for me to leave, it was storming, and I couldn't get out of Alaska. She had to call everybody to tell them the wedding would be delayed.

When the weather cleared up, I went to the Commander's Office, which nobody did. I asked him, "Is there any chance I could get out a couple of days early because I have a ride that will take me clear to Nebraska, and I won't have to buy a ticket to get home." He said, "Well, I'll talk to the Personnel Officer and let you know." He called me later and said my request had been approved, so I was released and transferred out of Kodiak two days earlier than scheduled. I rode on a military transport down to Seattle and then got a ride with a guy who was going to Bloomer, Wisconsin. He agreed to make a big swing around south to take me to North Platte, Nebraska.

His dad had sent him a new Ford car, and it had been

delivered to Whidbey Island. He had to go pick it up, buy the tag and have his papers signed while I got signed out. We drove his car straight through, not stopping except for gas till we got to North Platte. We were driving hard to get home because I didn't have much time to get there before the wedding.

We had to drive through snow that was about 8 inches deep. There were just tracks where the cars had been driving. He said, "I wish these people would get out of my way. I'm in a hurry! I'm going to show them how we drive in Alaska." He cut across the snow and started to go around the first car. His car fishtailed, and we went off the road and into the ditch. As we were sitting there, I kidded him and asked, "Tell me again how you're going to teach them how to drive?" He said, "Oh, shut up!" We were lucky. He put it in low, drove us out of that ditch, and we were on the road again going east on Highway 30. We took off after that and never stopped till we got to Nebraska.

Don Tustin, Harlan and Berniece met us in North Platte. I got out of the car, and the guy who brought me went on to Wisconsin. I walked up to where Berniece was. She was embarrassed, and I tried to get her over that right quick. Harlan's car was down the street, so we had a big kiss. We walked to the car and got in.

Harlan cut across country from North Platte and took the blacktop to Oakley where Wayne was waiting for me. He drove me straight to the courthouse in Gove where I needed to get the marriage license. After all that, we went out to the farm.

I had brought my dress blue uniform which was perfectly clean and ready for the wedding. Here's the funny part. After we ate supper, Mom said, "Sit down and give me your hand." She put clear polish on my fingernails. I think she was just nervous. She had spent some time in Oakley helping with the wedding preparations too.

The next morning, I got out of the bed in the southwest bedroom where I had slept. Since there was no heat in the bedroom, I was cold. As I walked into the dining room, I stepped right in the middle of the floor furnace not knowing that the grate was hot, and I burned both of my feet, but not bad enough to stop me.

Mom rode up to Oakley with someone else, so Wayne drove me there in her car, and we made it in time for the wedding. The preacher from Oakley married us in the Methodist Church on February 20, 1951. Wayne was my best man and Carolyn, Berniece's sister, was her maid of honor. The wedding was small, mostly just family.

Harlan had a Ford farm car that he let us use for our honeymoon to Denver. We stayed in a motel there. One of the things we did was to go to Buffalo Bill's grave up in the mountains. When our time was up, we came back to Oakley. I had a month's leave from the Navy.

Berniece was teaching school in Quinter at the time. She had a substitute teacher take her place for two weeks during our wedding and honeymoon. When we got back, Berniece had to go back to teaching, and we rented a room from some people in Quinter.

On the days she was teaching, I'd take her over to the schoolhouse, then go down to Gove and stay with Mom all day. I'd get back to Quinter in time to pick up Berniece after school. We'd either go out to eat or just stay home for the night.

When my leave was over, I met the guy from Bloomer, Wisconsin, and we started back for Whidbey Island where I had been reassigned. We took turns driving. At one point while I was driving, there was a baby wearing nothing but a diaper standing on the yellow line just ahead of us. I slammed on the brakes and asked the guy, "Is that a little baby?" He looked, and said, "Yeah." I stopped, got out of the car, and picked up the baby. A woman came running down a side road and said, "Oh, thank God he's alright!" Of course, I had my uniform on, and she thanked me. I guess the little dickens got outside and decided he needed to go somewhere, so he went over to the highway. He didn't even have any shoes on.

Berniece finished teaching that school term, and I got a ten day leave to go home to bring her back to Whidbey Island with me. We needed a car and had both saved money for one. I think I had about three or four hundred dollars. She bought a car for us, and I didn't see it till I got back home to Kansas. It was a used Ford coupe.

We went to her parents' house in Oakley where we had all kinds of presents that people had given us. After we had opened them, we stored them in the bedroom that had been hers. We took only the ones we thought we'd need, then headed off for Whidbey Island.

I had rented a summer place for us. I didn't think she'd like it. I kept telling her it wasn't very fancy. She said, "That's alright. We'll get by."

Our five-month honeymoon on Whidbey Island was

wonderful! The beach is nice up there in North Washington especially in the summertime. We had so much fun! We'd take some hotdogs, marshmallows and a can of beans or something like that and go down to the beach at night. We'd gather some rocks and make a little fire with driftwood. Berniece and I sat there and watched the sun go down in the west, and when it got down towards the ocean, there'd be an orange pathway that looked like a road that ran clear to the sun. When it got dark, we'd load up the car and go back home.

My job back at Whidbey was in the office working for the Lieutenant Commander. I'd do spread sheets that went to the galley and to the warehouses for airplane parts. I sat at my desk and did the paperwork on those. If my Lieutenant Commander wanted a letter, I would type it for him. I had to make carbon copies of it, and I couldn't make a mistake. I'd put his name on it with mine down at the bottom. When I'd take it into his office, he would change it almost every single time, then I'd have to do it over again.

As the Korean War continued, they started pulling a lot of us out of Whidbey to put us on an aircraft carrier that was headed for Japan to fight North Korea. I was an alternate on that list, but my name wasn't called. I was a short-timer, so I finished out the rest of my days at Whidbey working in the office. The officers assigned to the building kept trying to get me to re-enlist, but I said, "Nope, I'm going home!" That was the end of my Navy career.

TWENTY THREE
A SURPRISE VISIT

After I got out of the Navy, Berniece and I went back to Oakley. I got a job for twenty-eight days for a big farmer who lived west of town. I drove his truck and hauled milo into Winona and Oakley. Since I didn't have time to find a place to stay, we lived in the basement of Harlan and Lorane's house. After a bit, I said to Berniece, "Let's go back into the Navy." She said, "I don't want to do that." Harlan didn't want us to leave either.

During that time, a carload of my brothers and sisters came from Wichita to Oakley. In the car were my siblings, Bob, Hershel, Maryetta and Dorothy. Hershel's wife Bonnie, Dorothy's daughter Connie and Maryetta's daughters Allanna and Dianna came too. They wanted to surprise me.

They went first to Mom's house at the farm northwest of Gove. She told them I was living in Oakley with Harlan and Lorane, so they drove up there. When they met Berniece, they asked her if she thought I would want to see them. She said, "Yes."

When I came in from hauling milo, Berniece met me at the door. (My siblings had gone to eat somewhere in town, but Berniece kept it a secret that they were there in Oakley.) After Harlan, Lorane, Berniece and I ate supper, Berniece asked me to go take a shower. She surprised me then and told me that my siblings were coming back and wanted to meet me.

Mom called from Gove and talked to Berniece, then Berniece handed the phone to me. Mom told me, "Have them come here. I can put them all up at my house." We loaded up, and all of us went down to Gove. Harlan and Lorane came down for part of the evening too. Mom made room for all of us to stay overnight at the farm, and she got acquainted with them too. Maryetta had sent me pictures of my family while I was at Corpus Christi, so I knew what they looked like, but I didn't know them. They didn't feel like family because I was only three years old when I was thrown away.

The only sibling I remembered from my childhood was Bob. As I talked to him, one mystery from my childhood memory was solved. He told me that he was the one who had protected me when the other kids at the orphanage tried to take my toys away from me. He said, "I'd sit there with you all day and keep the other kids from stealing your toys." (I still have the little metal truck from that time. It's a treasure to me.) Bob also told me, "I remember the day you got in that big limousine. I looked out the window of the orphanage, and you were looking out the window of the car. We waved goodbye to each other."

My sisters, Maryetta and Dorothy, told me they were put in the Brown Home, on the west side of Abilene. That building (now the Lebold Mansion), was used as an orphanage from 1930 until around 1939. According to the children's workers, the girls were naughty, so they were placed in a tower above the house. (To this day, you can still see that tower.) It was cold in the wintertime, and they didn't have any heat. They were afraid they were going to freeze to death.

When my siblings and I were taken out of our home, Herbie was just a little baby. Some people who had a dairy up north took him. The dairyman's wife took care of him until all the rest of my siblings were brought back together.

We had relatives, an aunt May Guy (Walter's sister) and a cousin "Lexie" (Alexia) Lorson, who worked to try to get us removed from State custody and returned to our family. Years later, Berniece and I visited with Lexie Lorson. She told us she was originally made guardian for all of my siblings. Aunt May ran a boarding house in Wichita, and I think some of them might have stayed with her for a while, and the others stayed with Lexie.

I had already been sent out on the train and headed west to live with the Blands. Lexie was told by the Kansas Children's Home and Service League that Donnie had been adopted by a wealthy family in Western Kansas, and they would not give her any information as to my whereabouts.

In later years, Berniece and I got to meet and visit with Lexie's sister, "Loddie" (Lodisha) Bird. We got to know her a little bit and were able to piece together more information about my family.

It's amazing how God caused events to happen. During the late 1950's and early 1960's there were silos built to hold the Atlas Missiles for protection against Russia. My brother,

Bob, was working in one of those silos north of Wichita with a man named Gene Siemers from Gove. They didn't know each other at first, but they got acquainted while eating their lunch.

I guess Bob asked Gene where he was from. He said, "west Kansas." Bob told Gene that he had a brother who was taken out there as a young child. As they talked more and put two and two together, Gene told Bob, "I lived at his foster mother's house while I was in high school."

Gene was from down east of Harlan's farm in Missouri Flats (an area about ten miles south of Gove.) He and his sister stayed with Letia during school at Gove, and they "bached" upstairs in the sunroom.

Gene was drafted and was on a train headed for the service soon after school was out. I lost track of him and found out later that he was in an Airborne unit which parachuted all the time. After he got out of the service, he married Lois Bretz, a girl from west of Winona. They moved down to Wichita so he could work on the Atlas Missile silo there. That's how God's hand was at work in causing my brother, Bob, and Gene to meet each other.

———————

In a lot of ways my story is similar to that of children who were placed on the orphan train.* A pamphlet would

———

* The Orphan Train Movement was a supervised welfare program that transported children from crowded Eastern cities of the United States to foster homes largely in rural areas of the Midwest. The orphan trains operated between 1854 and 1929, relocating from about 200,000 children.[1]

be sent out saying that the orphan train would be coming to town. People would come to see the children, and they could decide which one they wanted to take.

I have a book called *Searching for Home* written by Martha Nelson Vogt and Christina Vogt.[2] The book is about orphans from three different families who rode the orphan train from New York City to Sterling, Abilene and McPherson, Kansas.

One of the orphan boys, Cliff Switzer, ended up in Kanorado, Kansas, in later life. When he was a kid, the guy who came up to check him out felt his arms to see how much muscle he had. The man wanted him only as a farm hand. When he thought Cliff should be doing more work, he beat him. The lady who ran the orphan train came down, found him and placed him on another farm where they treated him nicer.

I had the chance to get acquainted with Anna Fuchs, another one of the orphans on that train, when she gave a lecture at the local bank in McPherson. She and her two sisters were put on the train after their parents died of tuberculosis. Anna had a crippled hand, and she would hide it behind her so people wouldn't see it, because she knew if they did, they wouldn't want to take her. Sure enough, her little sisters were taken, and she was left standing there.

A spinster Sunday School teacher came up and said, "I'll take her." That lady put her through school and college. Anna worked for years at Alliance Insurance. She was later in a nursing home at Lindsborg, and when I talked to her, she told of all those things that had happened to her. When her adoptive mother got old, Anna went to court and was made guardian and caregiver for her own mother. Anna never married.

I asked her some very pointed questions. I didn't know if she would answer them, but she did. One of my questions was, "Do you ever have nightmares about the things you went through before you were adopted?" She said, "Yes, quite often." I asked, "How do you cope with that?" She said, "The only way I can do it is to think of all the good things that have happened to me since that time."

TWENTY FOUR
OUR OWN FARM

After we had been living with Berniece's parents for a while, Harlan made a deal with us that he said would make us a lot of money. He said, "I'll buy a farm and the machinery. You can run it, and we'll split the profit." He didn't look very long before he bought a farm up by Levant, Kansas. It had a basement house, and that's where we lived. We also had a barn, a chicken house and a tank house.

Harlan brought out only about seven head of cattle or so, as I recall. The first year, they got "bangs" (brucellosis). I didn't know what that was. I went to him and said, "You know those cattle you brought out? They're having their calves too early, and they don't even have any hair on them." He never replaced any of those cattle.

Berniece and I had great hopes while living on that place, but we struggled. I tried so many things just to make a living. I ran a road grader, operated a caterpillar with a loader on it and built seven stock trailers to try to sell. I couldn't sell those trailers. The only one that sold was to my neighbor, Gene Olson.

Another good friend and neighbor, Bob Lewallen, and

I pulled water wells in the area. I also started working with Bob and his brother-in-law, Bob Potter, building houses. We were making a profit, so I would put that money into cattle. I wanted to start building my herd of Black Angus cattle, so I'd buy registered Black Angus bred heifers, usually four at a time. Although Harlan preferred Herefords, I liked Angus cattle. I don't think he was too happy about that.

Something else Berniece and I did was to raise three or four hundred chickens to sell. I'd fill the coops with frying-sized chickens and take them into Oakley, Colby or wherever I could go to sell them. Some of the women in Oakley asked, "Can you kill them? We don't like to do that." I'd wring two chickens' necks at the same time, lay them down and say, "There you are." They'd say, "Thank you!"

―――――――

All three of our kids were born while we lived at the farm. When Berniece was expecting Donnie, I took her to town in our Ford car to go for her monthly doctor's check-up. It was coyote country around there where we lived. A big coyote came across the road in front of us and into a wheat field. I put that car into low gear, and away we went. I chased it in a circle. Berniece was screaming! One more circle, and I would have had the coyote, but she made me quit. I took her on to the doctor, and everything checked out okay.

When Donnie was born, Harlan came up to the hospital and said, "What are you going to name that boy?" I said,

"His name is Donald Earl Junior." Harlan said, "His name is Donald Harlan." I didn't like it, but that's the way it went.

It was wintertime, the ground was frozen, and I wrecked my truck. The door broke off, so I was driving it without the door. Donnie was about two or three years old and when he rode with me, he would get inside my arms while I was driving. He'd stand in the seat and would crowd right in beside me when I'd go the elevator at Winona. I got chicken feed there, and he would "help" with that.

Later when he was a little older and I was busy building houses, I'd call Berniece on the CB radio and tell her to have Donnie dressed and have his boots on because I'd be home in just a little bit to pick him up. We'd go fill the truck bed with silage before the snow came. He'd be ready, and the two of us would go down, fill up the truck, then drive back and put it in the shed. The next morning, I'd take him along if the weather was good, and we'd go out to the pasture and unload the silage to feed the cows.

I was busy trying to make a living, and I guess I overdid it, I don't know. Maybe I should have spent more time with him. He enjoyed going out with me to get the silage, I know that. He had a little three-tined pitchfork, and mine had four tines.

We had all those cattle, and the first time he saw me operating on those bull calves, he went into the house bawling. I had to talk to him, and he kinda got the idea.

Rob was born in Oakley too. When he was little, he learned a lot from watching Donnie. They rode the bus to school in Winona. He was little enough that he didn't have to feed the cows.

Somebody in Winona had some hamsters, and I got a couple of them for the boys. We kept them in the tank house or on the porch. The boys would play with them in the lawn. I remember that the hamsters had babies.

Marie's husband, Gail Beesley, invested in a whole bunch of Shetland ponies. We wintered some of them at our place. We used a couple of them for the boys to ride and train. Donnie's would pull a cart. Sometimes he would take his mom with him on a ride in that cart. Rob would stand in front of his pony eyeball to eyeball and say, "Now pony, you be nice to me, and I'll be nice to you." He learned to ride, but I don't think he exactly liked it. In the springtime, we took the ponies back to Gail because he had a buyer for them. We had trained them to ride, so he sold them.

I was with Berniece in Oakley when Jody was born. Everything was fine, and I headed to Winona to buy coffee for my friends. The way we did it back then was that when you had a new baby, you bought coffee for everyone at the cafe. I got there, and the lady running the cafe said, "Hey, Don, they just called from Oakley and said they need you down there at the hospital, and you're supposed to bring someone with type O blood as soon as possible." I was scared! I went up to Bob Potter's house and asked him if he could be a donor. He said he could. We picked up Harry Barnett too.

We headed toward Oakley. I was hitting about 100 miles per hour on the straight-away. I got there and pulled in. All three of us were scared to death! I went running in and said, "What's the problem?" The nurse said, "Nothing." I asked her why she wanted me to bring a blood donor. She said, "We just wanted you to replace the blood that Berniece needed." I said, "Lady, don't you ever do that again!" We could have gotten killed driving like I was! Dr. Marchbanks was the doctor, and when he found out what she had done, he chewed her out royally. The preacher said, "I thought for a while that I was going to die!"

———————

Sadie, a border collie, was our cattle dog. At one time, she got kicked in the mouth by a steer. I thought it was going to kill her. She ran over to a snowbank, and the snow turned red. It wasn't long till she was up, and from then on, she knew how to nip the cattle's heels without getting hurt.

There were times when I would be away working, and the cattle would get out. Berniece would have to get them back into the pasture, and she'd take Sadie along to help. Sadie did a very good job. Berniece would let her out of the car, and Sadie would go to work barking and nipping at their heels to get the cows back in.

———————

Sometimes Kenneth and I would help each other out during wheat harvest. He would bring his combine and truck up to our place. We had a great time working together. One thing we did just for fun was to throw our hats through the combine at the end of harvest. It became a tradition. Our hats were pretty worn out by that time anyway.

I'd put a stock tank in the back yard and fill it with water. After a long day in the field, we would jump in for a quick dip to cool off. Those were good memories. (I have a picture of Jody and me in that tank when she was just a little girl.)

One Halloween we invited Kenneth and Mae and their kids up for supper. They dressed up so we wouldn't recognize them. They knocked on the door, and when we answered it, we couldn't tell who they were. Kenneth and Mae were down on their knees with Boyd and Barbara standing behind them. Kenneth finally said, "Well, that's pretty good, you invite us up for supper and then when we get here, you don't even know us." We all had a big laugh over that. Kenneth was like our dad, Cliff. He loved to joke and have fun.

Sometimes we would play hide and seek together with the kids and relatives. One time, Kenneth and I were playing with the kids, and he climbed the wind charger tower to hide up on top. Boyd gave away Kenneth's hiding place when he looked up and said, "I know where my dad is." We'd hide all over the farm, underneath the tractor, in the granary or almost anywhere, then the others would have to find us. We had to run back and touch the tank house before the person that found us could get there in order to win. We made our own fun.

For the Fourth of July, we would get together with our neighbor, Bill Siruta and his family. Bill's bachelor brother would go to Nebraska to get the fireworks. They were bigger than what we could buy in Kansas. We'd enjoy shooting off the fireworks and then have some home-made ice cream.

***

At one time, when we were living at our farm, some of my Shugart siblings came for a visit. They brought their dad, Walter, with them. I had never met him, did not know him and had no feelings for him. He was never a father to me. We didn't really know how to talk to each other, didn't know what to say. I tried to talk to him, but the words just were not there. I remember him telling me he was sorry for what had happened in our family and that he had done the best he could. That was hard for me to accept.

TWENTY FIVE
MY BROTHER WAYNE

I was very close to my brother, Wayne. When I was living at the farm with Dad and Mom, Wayne and I would ride our horses to school. We would put them in Cooks' barn in the southwest part of Gove, later known as the Courtney place. (I quit riding to school because I didn't want Berniece to think I smelled like a stinking horse, so I started walking.)

Later, when Wayne was going to high school, he bought a brand-new Chevy truck. He went south and hauled wheat to pay for it, but I don't know who he went with.

He had a car too. It was a 1949 or '50 green sedan. The first time I saw it, he was coming from the east to our place. I had unhooked the cultivator and was coming across the pasture with the tractor and heading to the house. He came screaming up that sanded road, dirt fogging everywhere. He raced up the driveway, and when I looked up, here he tore out though the gate and into the pasture. He was romping it coming right straight for me. When he got close to me, he slid around, jumped out and said, "Hi, how you doin?" I said, "That's a new car!"

He had a horse named Newt. When Wayne wanted to haul him somewhere and didn't want to put the stock racks on the truck, he'd back up to a ditch and raise the hoist a little bit. He had trained that horse to jump up into the back of the truck with just the grain box on it. He'd let the bed down, and you'd see him driving off with that horse just standing there. Newt didn't try to jump out or anything. He loved to ride in the truck like that.

Wayne was always pulling something. After Berniece and I were married, Elinor decided she was going to have a family get-together. Because it was such a nice night, we were going to sleep outside on the west side of Elinor and Lawrence's house (the former Joe Losey place.) Wayne was there, and we were talking. We started telling ghost stories to the nieces and nephews. Half of them were scared and being very vocal about it. Marie and Gail's daughter Linda was one of them.

I whispered to Wayne, "Let's scare the heck out of this bunch of kids." The kids and I got into a vehicle and drove out east of Gove to the Andy Peirano place, a brick house that had been vacant for years. The story goes that he built it for his intended wife, but she wouldn't marry him, so it was never lived in.

Wayne and his friend, Wayne Packard, jumped into his pickup and took off ahead of us. They got inside that house and went up to the second floor. I took the kids in there, and about that time, Wayne started making weird noises. I'm not sure that no one wet their pants.

There was red paint on the stairway where someone had splashed it. How it got there, I don't know, but if you took a flashlight, it looked like blood running down the side of that wall. The kids were "bent out of shape" and wouldn't go near that house again.

Wayne was later drafted into the Army and was stationed in Massachusetts. While he was there, he met and married Marion Wilson. Berniece and I went to their wedding in Boston along with Kenneth, Mae and Mom. Wayne and Marion moved back to Gove in 1958.

Another crazy thing Wayne did was that he drove an old junk car off the bluff west of Mom's house at the farm. He wanted to make it look like he went over the bluff inside the car, so we used my movie camera to film him. When he got close to the edge, he opened the door and jumped out, but I stopped filming just before that. The car crashed to the bottom. Wayne went down, got inside, and I started filming again as he crawled out. The funny part was that even after that, he was able to start the car, so he brought it back up and drove it off the bluff again. It was demolished that time.

TWENTY SIX

HARRY BARNETT

Harry Barnett was a pastor who moved to Winona with his wife and kids. He said he had come to Winona from Asbury Seminary in Wilmore, Kentucky, by Divine appointment. At that time in my life, I didn't know what Divine appointment meant.

He said he liked to hunt, and he wanted to come out to my place to do that. It wasn't till years later that I realized he was mainly there to hunt souls. He'd come into the house and say to Berniece, "Have you got a chicken leg in the refrigerator?" She would say, "Yes." She'd fry two or three chickens at a time so there would be plenty of leftovers. He'd grab a chicken leg, and we'd head out. We'd go hunting, and the conversation would turn to the Lord, the church and spiritual things like that.

Before Harry was saved, he served in the Army and was in Belgium. During that time, the Americans were overrun by the Germans at the siege of Bastogne. They were surrounded by tanks and couldn't get away. The Germans would use spotters to come in and shoot one or two of the Americans and then they'd run back out. (Anybody that has been in the service knows something of this story.)

It had been cloudy for days which made the fighting difficult. Harry got sick, and he knelt down on a log that was in his path and prayed, "Lord, if You get me out of here, I'll serve You the rest of my life." He said when he got up, God had caused the sun to come out enabling them to be able to see to fight.

While Harry was there, God blessed Patton. (Patton was the general that Eisenhower reprimanded because of some of his actions and some of his inflammatory remarks.) General Patton was stranded in France, but suddenly he was given orders over the radio to get his whole army to Belgium. The news we got here at home was that Belgium was surrounded by Germans, and all of our men were going to get killed. Patton started out, cranked those soldiers into gear and told them to get on the stick and get going.

Three days later at sunup Patton was in Bastogne. Because it had been dark, the Germans did not know that he had brought his whole army in from France. When he arrived, the Germans were petrified because they didn't have any gas left in their tanks. Patton had filled up his tanks before he left France. The next day, the sun came out. Well, the sun was the biggest thing because Belgium had not had a sunny day, and the Germans didn't know how to fight this battle. God truly blessed Patton! God answered Harry's prayer and got him out of Belgium.

Fast forward to Pier 91. That was a gateway to Alaska, both for the Navy and the flood of people going there to homestead. Harry said, "I was sitting at Pier 91 in Seattle. It was a nice, sunny day, and I was thinking how great it was going to be to go to Alaska." A voice said, "Harry, you didn't keep your promise." He looked around, and there was nobody on the pier but him. The seats were all empty. He sat there for a little bit, and again a voice said, "Harry, you didn't keep your promise." Then it hit him. He had bought a ticket to go to Alaska to live. When he heard the voice the second time, he knew Who it was. Harry said he went inside, turned in his ticket and booked a trip back to Asbury Seminary in Wilmore, Kentucky. He wasn't quite done with his training, so he finished it, got his diploma and was ready to head out. God directed him to preach and tell people about the Lord Jesus Christ. That's how he was sent to Winona. When the pastor of the Methodist Church at Winona left, Harry took that position.

He told a story of an Indian guy at Asbury by the name of Big Foot. Big Foot really believed in prayer! Harry had taken it upon himself while he was there to try to help a young man who would drink and then come into the dorm. He said Big Foot would sit out there under the eaves of Asbury Seminary dormitory and pray all night long for that guy.

Harry really was my spiritual mentor. He would come out to our house many, many, many times. He and I would sit and talk about spiritual things.

Berniece, the kids and I started attending the Methodist Church in Winona, which he pastored. Berniece repented of her sin, trusted Christ as her Savior and surrendered her life to Him in 1962 at one of the Easter Services there at the church.

TWENTY SEVEN
ADOPTED INTO GOD'S FAMILY

In September 1962, we had a revival service in our church. The evangelist was Jimmy Lentz. He had gone through Asbury Seminary too and was a missionary to Mexico. He had promised Harry Barnett that wherever Harry was when he became a pastor, he would come and hold a revival service at his church, so he kept his promise and came to Winona. On Sunday and Monday, we loaded up and took our family to church.

On Monday night, my friend and neighbor, Bob Lewallen, was not there. I called him and asked him why he wasn't at church. He asked, "Do you want to talk?" I said, "Well, I guess so." I hung up and told Berniece, "Something's the matter with Bob." The next morning, I took care of my cattle, got in the pickup and met him halfway between my place and his. It was a foggy morning. We pulled off to the side of the country road and sat there and tried to figure out what was happening with us. We both decided we needed to be at church early that night to talk to that evangelist and Harry. So when we got there and went in, Harry's wife, Gladys, said the men were in the basement praying.

We went downstairs, and there they were, praying for the service. I've always said they prayed "around the world" before they acknowledged that we were there. They finally turned to us and said, "Oh, guys, what do you want?" We both looked at the evangelist and said, "We need something. We're short something." He said, "Have you asked the Lord into your life? Have you confessed to Him that you're a sinner?" Harry looked at us and said, "What do you want God to do, hit you over the head with a two-by-four?" (When he said that, it spoke to both of us because we'd been building houses and were using lots of two-by-fours.) Harry and Jimmy Lentz went through the four spiritual laws with us. We prayed, confessed our sins and committed our lives to the Lord. At that moment, the darkness fell off, and we stood there in the basement of that church knowing something had happened to us. They told us that God had accepted us as His children, and we finally believed that He had. "All that the Father gives Me shall come to Me; and the one who comes to Me I will certainly not cast out" (John 6:37). We were both overjoyed knowing that Jesus had saved us from our sin!

We went upstairs, and Wilma Fletcher who had come from Northern Nebraska to be a special singer was singing "A New Name in Glory." I identified with that song because it tells that once I was a sinner, but when I received a free pardon from the Lord Jesus Christ and came to him, my name was written down in glory. I'm so thankful that my sins were forgiven, and I am on my way to heaven where the angels sang of my redemption.

I also love the song by David Sapp, "There is a River." It

tells of a river that flows from deep within and the fountain that frees our souls from sin. Jesus calls us to come to that vast supply of Living Water which will never run dry. These songs ministered to my thirsty soul.

That was the day I met the Lord Jesus Christ personally. I became a child of the King because I was finally adopted… not into an earthly family but into God's eternal family. I finally had a Father who would NEVER DIE NOR EVER LEAVE ME.

We invited Kenneth and his family from Gove to come the fifty-six miles to Winona to attend one of the services that week. That night Boyd and Barbara both accepted Jesus Christ as their Savior. Mae was already a Christian. I don't know when Kenneth accepted the Lord.

From that day on, we served our Lord, led other people to Christ and shared our testimonies with them. During the time in Winona, we joined the church and were active there. Jesus Christ has been in my life ever since. The following story reminds me of the bummer lambs I raised when I was young and how Jesus became my Great Shepherd when I was broken and rejected. I'm so grateful for His love!

"THE BUMMER LAMB"
By Steve Adams

Every once in a while, a ewe will give birth to a lamb and rejects it. There are many reasons she may do this. If the lamb is returned to the ewe, the mother may even kick the poor animal away. Once a ewe rejects one of her lambs, she will never change her mind.

These little lambs will hang their heads so low that it looks like something is wrong with its neck. Their spirit is broken.

These lambs are called "bummer lambs." Unless the shepherd intervenes, that lamb will die, rejected and alone. So. Do you know what the shepherd does?

He takes that rejected little one into his home, hand-feeds it and keeps it warm by the fire. He will wrap it up with blankets and hold it to his chest so the bummer can hear his heartbeat. Once the lamb is strong enough, the shepherd will place it back in the field with the rest of the flock.

But that sheep never forgets how the shepherd cared for him when his mother rejected him. When the shepherd calls for the flock, guess who runs to him first?

That is right, the bummer sheep. He knows his voice intimately.

It is not that the bummer lamb is loved more, it just knows intimately the one who loves it.

It's not that it is loved more, it just believes it because it has experienced that love one on one.

So many of us are bummer lambs, rejected and broken. But He is the good Shepherd. He cares for our every need and holds us close to His heart so we can hear His heartbeat.

We may be broken but we are deeply loved by the Shepherd.

"'The Lord is my shepherd; I shall not want.

He maketh me to lie down in green pastures: He leadeth me beside the still waters.

He restoreth my soul: He leadeth me in the paths of righteousness for his name's sake.

Yea, though I walk through the valley of the shadow of

death, I will fear no evil: for Thou art with me; Thy rod and Thy staff they comfort me.

Thou preparest a table before me in the presence of mine enemies: Thou anointest my head with oil; my cup runneth over.

Surely goodness and mercy shall follow me all the days of my life, and I will dwell in the house of the Lord forever"' (Psalm 23 KJV).[1]

TWENTY EIGHT
UPROOTED AND DEVASTATED

Although I had become a child of God, things continued to grow worse on the farm both financially and in our relationship with Harlan. Our agreement was that we would split the profit from the farm, but there was no profit. We went to Oakley to see Harlan and Lorane. Harlan and I had some terrible words. Berniece and her mother were standing there crying their eyes out. Our relationship went downhill from there. That was the beginning of the end of our life in Kansas. When Harlan acted the way he did, Berniece walked out of his house without even looking back. I was thankful she stuck by me! Harlan was not a good father-in-law to me, but Lorane was very good to both Berniece and me.

Finally, Berniece and I decided the best thing for us to do was to sell out and move away. As we prayed and considered where to go, God brought Denver to our minds. Berniece had gone to college there, and she liked Colorado. Also, Mom's foster sister, Aunt Eva Kline, and her family lived in the Denver area. (Aunt Eva was the mother of Chuck, Glen, Don, Jesse and Annette.)

I was hoping to be able to make a living as an electrician. I wrote a letter to the Colorado State Electrical Board to find out what was necessary to get my electrical license. They responded that I would need to take a test for my journeyman's license. I chose a date for the test.

We put our farm up for auction, and when it was over we had hardly anything left. Berniece and I were both exhausted. Although we had built our house and made improvements at the farm, we lost the house and never got paid for it.

Our friends and neighbors, Gene and Dee Olson, came over to help pack up our things in their farm truck and got ready to move us to Denver. Gene wouldn't charge us anything for their help. We need more people like them in this world. They were sure there for us.

That night when we got packed up, it started to rain. It hadn't rained all summer. That was interesting.

Berniece drove the car, and I drove our pickup. I cried the whole way to Denver and asked, "Why me, Lord? I gave You my life. I belong to You. I've lost everything, and I don't have any money." But…He had a different plan. He was there and was with me all the way. It wasn't till years later that I realized He'd already made the way for us to move to Colorado, but we just didn't know it at the time. God Himself had a place for us to live and a new occupation for me. He was watching over us and put people in our path to help us.

When we got to Denver, we drove to Aunt Eva's daughter Annette's house. She helped us by calling her brother Chuck and asking him about a place for us to live. (I didn't know Chuck that well at the time, but I certainly got to know him very well later.) He was a contractor and had built thirteen houses to sell. She turned around and told me that he said, "Have him go over to the show home in Lakewood on West Mexico. I can't sell the [blankety-blank] thing anyway." What an answer to prayer and relief that was to us! We went over to the house, and with the help of the Olsons, started unloading our things. They stayed overnight with us.

The next morning, I went down to the State Capitol Building to take the test for my electrical license. A lot of other guys were there for the same reason. As we were standing outside in line, I noticed they were each carrying a book. I asked a guy, "What's the book for?" He looked at me kinda seriously and said, "Well, it's the *National Electrical Code Book*, and you need one for the test." I asked him where I could get one, and he told me there was a bookstore across the street.

I took off running, went inside the store and asked the lady, "Do you happen to have a copy of the *National Electrical Code Book*?" She said, "I don't know. We're about out, but I'll look." She came back with the only copy she had left, a paperback. I asked her how much it was. She told me $1.00. I gave her a dollar and quickly headed back to the Capitol Building.

When the proctor handed out the packets, I prayed and told the Lord that if He wanted me to be an electrician in Colorado, He was going to have to help me because I couldn't do it on my own. There were three booklets that we had to complete. One of them was open-book, so I was able to look up the answers that I needed. Another one was multiple choice and true or false where I had to fill in the circle for the correct answer. As I looked down the page, for each question, there was one circle that was darker than the others. I just went down the line filling in those dark circles. I think we were allowed two hours to finish. I was one of the first ones done, so I handed in my test to the proctor, and he asked, "You're not done already, are you?" I said, "I've done the best I could. I don't know any more." He asked, "Did you look it over?" I said, "I don't need to. That's all I can do."

God led me all the way. I love the words to the following song:

"I WILL PILOT THEE"
Words and Music by Mrs. Emily D. Wilson
Copyright 1927
Under Public Domain

Sometimes when my faith would falter
And no sunlight I can see,
I just lift mine eyes to Jesus
And I whisper, "Pilot me."

Refrain:
Fear thou not, for I'll be with thee,
I will still thy Pilot be;
Never mind the tossing billows,
Take my hand and trust in Me.

Often, when my soul is weary
And the days seem, oh, so long,
I just look up to my Pilot
And I hear this blessed song: [Refrain]

When temptations round me gather
And I almost lose my way,
Somehow, in the raging tempest,
I can hear my Saviour say: [Refrain]

When I come to Jordan's river
And its troubled waters see,
On the brink I'll see my Saviour
And I know He'll pilot me. [Refrain].[1]

When I finished there, I got in my red Ford pickup and went back over to the house to help finish unloading the truck and then said goodbye to the Olsons. That was our start in Denver. God was clearly leading us, and He put people in our lives to help us. Besides the Olsons, Annette and Chuck were the first ones.

I went over to see Chuck not long after that. He hired me to help him frame up a house he was building. He paid me $3.00 an hour, and I thought I'd died and gone to heaven.

One day it was supposed to snow, and I was nervous about the weather holding things up. He said to me, "Don, you don't have any cattle to get in and feed. You're going to go home and sit down and watch TV. By noon, the snow will all be gone, and we'll be back working." He was right!

Chuck told me not to be disappointed if I didn't pass that electrical test the first time because most people have to take it more than once. God was good! I passed it with the first try and got my journeyman's license while I was working on that house with Chuck. God did that for me! I know it was Him.

I worked for Chuck for about two weeks, and when I was done with the house, I went out to see if I could find a job. I told Berniece to pray, and I would check with all the contractors. Unbeknownst to me, Denver was a union town, and nobody would talk to me because I wasn't union.

I went by the office of a guy named Benton Tibbetts who was attending Southern Gables Free Methodist Church in Lakewood where we had started going. He said, "Gene Houston told me that if you stopped by here, he wanted you to come talk to him." I drove over there to see him.

Gene introduced himself and said, "I can't figure this out. I've been working on Texaco pumps for years, installing, removing, putting in bigger ones and everything. A while back a pastor came by and wanted me to bid the electrical job for a church in Golden, but I didn't think I'd get it. I just did it as a favor to him. That was in March, and here it is fall. I just found out I got the bid, and I don't have anybody to help me. Would you like to do that job?" I said, "I'm not that good at wiring. I know a little bit but not a lot. I wired my mom's outbuildings at the farm in Kansas, but that's about all." He said, "That's all right. I'll teach you."

I went to work for him, and, like Chuck, he paid me $3.00 an hour. Every day at noon, we'd take our dinner pails, get in his truck, pray and sit there eating our lunch. As we did, we'd go chapter by chapter through the electrical code book. He would say, "If there's something you don't know, ask me tomorrow." I don't remember how many months that took, but we finally got the church done. He said, "Well, Don, thank you for helping me out, but I'm sorry, I don't have any more for you to do right now." I said, "Thank you for the work and for all the information you've given me." Because of Gene Houston and that book, God got me through.

I was out looking for work again, and God answered in a difficult way. It had been only two or three days after wiring the church for Gene when he called me. He told me that while he was working on a Texaco sign, he was on a ladder that was on ice. It slipped out from under him, and he went crashing down and broke both wrists. He asked me to come over to talk to him. When I got to his place, he said, "I want you to run my company." I said, "I can't do that." He said, "Yes, you can. My wife and I will be sitting here, and if you run into trouble, you call me, and I'll tell you what to do." That's the way God works. I worked another two and a half or three months for Gene. He finally healed enough so he could drive the truck with his broken wrists, and again I had to say "Goodbye."

Sometime after that, he speculated on building low-income housing in Denver. He bid the job too low and lost his shirt because of it. He went bankrupt and was ashamed of that.

Later he moved over to the Western Slope to Ouray where he bought a two-wheeled trailer to pull behind his pickup. He'd take the overlay off uranium ore with a slip and then haul the ore into Ouray with his pickup and trailer to the uranium mill. They'd weigh it, he'd sell it, and that's how he'd make his living.

I found out sometime later that he got cancer from working with the uranium. I never got to talk to him again. When I heard how bad his cancer was, I wrote him a letter telling him how thankful I was for what he had done for me when I worked for him.

After about two months, I got a letter from his wife. I didn't know he had passed away, but she told me when he got my letter, he was full of smiles. She said, "Gene was so happy to hear from you. He appreciated what you did for him. Before he died, he came to the point of no longer feeling guilty over going bankrupt." I was so thankful for Gene. He taught me how to be an electrician, and I'll never forget that! I'm reminded again of how God works.

TWENTY NINE

GOD'S BUSINESS — BLAND ELECTRIC

Jay Mitchell and I were both ushers at the Free Methodist Church in Lakewood. One Sunday as I was talking to him, I told him I'd like to start my own electrical company, but I didn't have enough money to do that. He asked me what I needed, and I told him I needed to buy a truck and electrical supplies. He told me to meet him in the parking lot of the Jefferson County Bank the next morning.

I drove to the bank like he asked. He took me inside and introduced me to the bank president then turned around and left. The president asked me how I knew Jay. I told him he was a friend of mine and that we went to the same church. He said, "What can I do for you?" I told him I needed $5,000 to start an electrical company. He asked if that was enough. I said, "Yea, and I'll pay it back as soon as possible." He set up a loan for six months with my Ford pickup as collateral. That was the start of my company, Bland Electric. (Praise the Lord, in two months I was able to write a check to pay off that loan.)

After I got the loan, I went to the Ford dealership and bought a service truck. It was interesting to me that the salesman was from Monument, Kansas, which is only about fourteen miles from Winona. That man had moved to Denver shortly before I did. I was thankful that God put someone from home in my path.

I bought electrical supplies from a wholesale distributor that I had done business with while working for Gene Houston. I had "Bland Electric" decals made for the sides of my truck.

When that was done, I went over to see Chuck to tell him that I had been able to buy a truck and get set up. He said I could wire his six-plex that was about a half mile from the house on West Mexico where we were living. That six-unit apartment building was the first big electrical and public service job I did in Colorado.

At that time, I was in the process of buying the show home from Chuck with my GI loan. I didn't even know about a GI loan until he told me, and he even filled out the paperwork for me. He took care of that, and I was able to make payments on the house that way.

Bill West was Chuck's foreman. When I needed something for my work, he would tell me where in town to get it. He was so helpful that way. I regretted that I didn't talk to him about the Lord at that time.

Because of some medical problem, Bill had to have his legs amputated. Later in life, I called him and asked if he would have coffee with me. He said, "Yes." We met at the Dairy Queen. As I talked to him, I said, "You know, I'm sorry, but I never told you about the best friend I ever had in the world." He asked, "Who's that?" I said, "He's Jesus Christ. I wouldn't be an electrician today if it wasn't for

Him. I gave my life to him in September 1962, and He's led me ever since." He shed a few tears, and I told him he could have the same assurance of eternal life if he'd just ask for His forgiveness and give his life to Him.

I finished wiring the six-plex for Chuck and needed to find more work. Before going out the door, I asked Berniece to pray. I went to several housing developers to see if they had any jobs for me to bid. I heard that Paul Walden of Nedlaw Construction Company was building a beauty shop on West Colfax, so I went to his office to see him. (Nedlaw is Walden spelled backwards.)

Again, I saw God's hand in the details. Paul's secretary was a Beougher from Orion, Kansas, just twelve miles west of Gove. I knew her family. I asked her if I could talk to Mr. Walden. She said, "No, he's busy." He was putting together contracts on a job of fifty-six condos and another with 275 condos. I said, "I just want a minute." She came back and said he would see me. I went in and told him, "My name is Don Bland, Mr. Walden." He said, "Call me Paul." I said, "I'm an electrician, and I'd like to bid your beauty shop." He said to me, "I've got the plans somewhere. Yeah, here they are. Give me a figure." I went home and went to work on the bid. As always, Berniece was praying. When I came up with the amount, I felt led to take $50 off the price. I went back downstairs to my office to make that change.

When I took my bid back to his office, he looked at it, and said, "Well, you're just about $50 under the lowest bid. You've got the job, but can you wait, and I'll draw you up a contract?" I said, "I can do that." What a wonderful God to lead me that way!

I did work for him for years. I'd bid his work and get it. I was able to rent an office from him. Years later, he'd just send his man down that hallway to my office with a bid sheet that he'd already made out with my name on it. He'd say, "Sign right here." I'd say, "Am I going to make any money?" He'd say, "You're going to make a lot of money."

My last job with Paul and Nedlaw Construction Company was a shopping center in Northglenn. He did the complete shopping center, a strip mall. It was the biggest one in Northglenn. God was good to me, and I praise His name!

One of the greatest blessings of my business was that both of my sons, Donnie and Rob, worked with me. In the early days of the business, we had to pull feeders into six feeder housings for the future tenants. I got everything together, but I didn't have the tools I needed. We decided we'd have to improvise. We tied all the cables together. Each one of them had four strands of high voltage wire. We tied them to the bumper of the pickup to pull them through the conduit. As we were pulling them, the Mexican men that the contractor had hired to run the concrete were there watching us. Things were going well, and I was very pleased with the progress. About half-way through, Rob said to me, "Dad, those guys are laughing at you." I asked, "What do you mean?" He said, "You're chewing your gum as fast as you're pulling these cables." After I gave my life to the Lord, I gave up cigarettes and replaced them with gum. Well, I didn't want to be laughed at, so I quit chewing gum.

One instance I remember was that as Rob was working

on a pre-stressed concrete building, the cable that held the scaffolding platform broke, and the platform came down right beside him. He wasn't hurt, but the guy that was on the platform was killed. That had quite an effect on Rob! At that time, I tried to get him to quit the electrical business, but he didn't want to. He loved it, and he continued with it. He was the youngest electrical journeyman to have a license in Colorado at that time. I was proud of him.

Other family members worked for me from time to time. My cousin, Don Kline, worked for a while running a trencher. My nephew, Marvin Beesley, ran that same trencher for me for a couple of weeks after he came back from Vietnam.

Another interesting thing that happened when I had my electrical business was that Donnie and I went downtown to 417 West Fourth Avenue, close to the Capitol to wire a building that somebody had bought to convert from a store into two apartments. We were looking at it to see what we had to do to put in new double service electric, one for the top and one for the bottom. Donnie said, "That picture of Grandpa Johnson standing in front of his grocery store in Denver looks just like this." Donnie had seen the picture at Mom's. We got the picture, brought it back to Denver and discovered it was the very same building.

Loving history, Donnie and I felt honored to wire an old building on Fourth Avenue that had belonged to Andrew Johnson, Mom's dad. We verified it by checking it at the Register of Deeds Office. It blew me away that I was bidding a job on a building that had belonged to him, and I hadn't even known it. It felt good to know that we had worked on the same wood that a relative from the distant past had also worked on. It was God who caused that to happen.

Aunt Eva told me more of what she knew about it, but she had never seen the store. I think Donnie took her down there to see the building that Andrew Johnson, her foster dad, had owned. I wish I knew more about his life, but Mom is not here to tell me.

Let me digress a little bit to tell you what I do know about Grandpa and Grandma (Anna) Johnson. I vaguely remember Grandpa Johnson. He was very tall and didn't talk much. He was a kind man. The reason I know he was kind is because he and Grandma Johnson took Aunt Eva in when she was just a baby and raised her as their own daughter. Her mother, Ellen, Grandma Johnson's sister, had died leaving Aunt Eva in need of care.

There's a family story about Grandpa Johnson going from the family homestead near Zurich, Kansas, to Colorado around 1879 to find work. He got a job helping put in the railroad that went through South Park and Royal Gorge. While he was there, he got word that his mother, Christina Hunt, was sick, and he thought he'd better get back home. (You have to remember there were no paved roads or automobiles like we have today.) He started walking, and when his shoes wore out, he wrapped burlap gunny sacks around his feet. I don't know how many days it took, but he walked the whole way from Royal Gorge to Zurich, Kansas. His mother was still alive, and he made it there in time to be with her.

He and his half-brother, Otto Hunt, later owned a store in Natoma, Kansas, called Johnson and Hunt General Merchandise. Grandpa evidently had health problems, and the doctor told him that his and Grandma Johnson's health would improve if they moved a little farther west to Gove County where the climate was better. Grandpa traded the store for a half section of land three miles northwest of Gove.

He built a beautiful two-story house for Grandma on their property. Grandpa Johnson put carbide lamps in their new house. Those were fascinating things in those days. They were powered by the reaction of carbide with water, creating acetylene gas which would then be piped into the house to the lamps. Grandpa had a big tank buried out by the wash house. To keep the pressure on the gas, he had a weighted float on it. As the gas would fill up in the tank, it would push the float down and the gas would flow through the pipes.

The lamp fixtures hanging in the center of the room were ornate. Some of the rooms had three of four fixtures including those mounted on the walls. They were beautiful! They had frosted glass, and some had flowers painted on them. Each of the fixtures had an igniter that you would pull with your finger. It would throw a spark which would ignite the gas. Later when Sanford Powers wired the house for electricity, he ran the wire right through those gas lines.

I asked Grandma Johnson one time, "Why did you pick Gove County to homestead? Couldn't you have found some place with trees?" She told Wayne and me that when they moved over there from Natoma, the grass in the draws was three to four feet tall in the summertime. They would cut it with a scythe, stack it with pitch forks, and that's what they used to feed their horses and cattle. Year after year, it slowly got shorter, but in those early years, they didn't have to plant cane. They harvested hay in their draws around there. The grass was tall for that area, and it was so nice!

Grandma Johnson had a wash house in the back yard. She had a double tub and one of them had a wringer on it. To heat her wash water, she would put a big kettle on top of her little wood-burning stove which was inside the wash house.

We went to Plainville one time after I came into the family. We put flowers on the family graves then went over to see Grandma Johnson's sister, Dollie Winters, and her husband, Willard.

I remember the sugar cookies that Grandma Johnson made and kept in her pantry. We never could exactly figure out the recipe. They were made with sour cream. That's what made them so good. We'd sit and talk to her while we ate cookies. She was quite a cook and quite a lady!

Now, back to Bland Electric. One day, I was over in Aurora bidding a job. As I was coming back, I saw smoke on the west side of Denver. I thought, "That's pretty close to one of my jobs." When I got closer, I realized it was in the big housing development that I was wiring for Ned-law. One of my workers (who was from Central College in McPherson) came running to me and said, "I pulled the trailer away from the project so it wouldn't catch on fire."

The Local 68 union wanted to put me out of business, and they burned down three of my projects. They didn't want a non-union electrician in Colorado, and I would not bow to them. I told them that God was taking care of me. They just laughed. A guy from the union came and talked to all of my men. The men that worked for me were so good, and I could trust each one of them. It wasn't long before the Colorado Bureau of Investigation caught the union men who had set the fires. They got fourteen years in the state pen.

When we decided to close our business, I told my guys and even my own sons to go downtown and get their unemployment checks. I said, "You deserve it." Three of my good men came to me and said, "Mr. Bland, if you'll keep your company going, we'll work for five dollars an hour less. We don't want to go down to the Unemployment Office where people are getting their money for free." I said, "I'm sorry guys, but I've already made my decision." They eventually did go, but my sons wouldn't do that.

It was a tough time as I sold everything, but God was as great as He could be to us! Bland Electric was a successful company. The success wasn't through me or my sons, but by trusting the Lord and doing what He led me to do. He guided us along. God is faithful!

Jay Mitchell, who helped me get my company started, became one of my best friends. When he was on his death bed, I went back to Colorado to see him. (By that time, we had retired and moved back to Kansas.) We spent probably an hour and a half talking about our lives and what God meant to us. As he was laying there in bed, he said, "I only regret one thing, and that is that I didn't tell more people about Jesus Christ and what His saving power would do." I said, "Jay, you don't have anything to feel bad about because you've built churches, dormitories and hospitals all over the west, and you gave most of your money away. You were a success, not just in our eyes, but in God's eyes because you've been so grateful and generous. He's got a special place for you." I told him goodbye and said, "I'll see you in heaven."

He died shortly after that. His son called and asked me to be a pallbearer if I could come out to Colorado to do that. I told him I would. When we got there, the pallbearers were lined up. There were five very distinguished men and one ol' Kansas farm boy named Don Bland. Jay's son said, "We knew we could count on you."

That was some of the time we had in Denver. We were successful in our business, and through it all, I found that my salvation was to be used to share His message with other people. That's the part I remember most.

THIRTY

AIRPLANES — MY JOY

From the time I was young and built those little airplanes out of balsa wood and sat in the cockpit of the plane that landed by Letia's house in Gove, I wanted to fly. Flying was an important part of my life. When I was living in Denver, I did a check ride to get my pilot's license changed over from military to civilian. Later I took another check ride to do mountain flying which is the most dangerous flying there is! The guy that approved me said that sometimes people would fly right into the side of the mountains because of the down drafts.

I wanted to buy an airplane, but I didn't have the money until after I had my own business in Colorado. God provided one right there in front of me, a 172 Cessna. It had been sitting for a long time, so I had it checked out to see if it was a good buy. It was good news when I was told there was nothing wrong with it. I was able to buy that first plane for five or six thousand dollars. That's when I started flying on my own. I really got a lot of enjoyment out of it! The poem *High Flight* is the way I felt when I was up in a plane.

"High Flight"
By John Gillespie Magee, Jr.

"A sonnet written by John Gillespie Magee, an
American pilot with the Royal Canadian Air Force in the
Second World War. He came to Britain, flew in a Spitfire
squadron, and was killed at the age of nineteen on
11 December 1941 during a training flight from the
airfield near Scopwick.)
Portions Of This Lovely Poem Appear On The
Headstones Of Many Interred In
Arlington National Cemetery,
Particularly Aviators And Astronauts"
(Above paragraph written by Michael Robert Patterson)

Oh! I have slipped the surly bonds of earth,
And danced the skies on laughter-silvered wings;
Sunward I've climbed and joined the tumbling mirth
of sun-split clouds — and done a hundred things
You have not dreamed of — wheeled and soared and swung
High in the sunlit silence. Hov'ring there,
I've chased the shouting wind along, and flung
My eager craft through footless halls of air.

Up, up the long delirious burning blue
I've topped the wind-swept heights with easy grace,
Where never lark, or even eagle, flew —
And, while with silent, lifting mind I've trod
The high untrespassed sanctity of space,
Put out my hand and touched the face of God.[1]

One time, Berniece and I were flying back to Kansas to a Tustin family reunion. We flew over our old house north of Winona. When we flew over Gene Olson's house, I poured the power to it and went straight up. Berniece said, "Oooooooohhhhhh, Lord! Mr. Bland, if you ever do that again, I'm not going to ride with you anymore!" It scared her to death! I never did that with her again.

Another time we flew out to Winona, ate lunch with our friends, Bob and Jeannine Lewallen, then headed on east. I landed at an airport in Salina then went down to McPherson for a meeting. (I was on the Board of Trustees of Central Christian College at that time.)

My good friend, Pastor Jim Means, had to go out to Brush, Colorado one time to hold a service for the church there. He didn't want to have to drive all the way, so I flew him out early on a Sunday morning. He held the service, and I sat and listened. They served us a light meal afterward then we got back in my plane and flew home. I'd have done that every week if I could have. I'd take him wherever he needed to go. Berniece would go with me too if it wasn't too far away.

Jody was my "flying buddy." She liked to go with me. We would go down east of Colorado Springs, make a big circle and come back. One time, we ran into a hailstorm south of Denver. She just sat beside me and held onto my arm. I got away from the storm by flying west toward the mountains and then back to the airport on the east side of Denver. Another time, we flew down east of Colorado Springs and went to a county fair. We landed at the airport, went to the fair and then flew back home.

I sold that first Cessna and bought my second airplane, a 182 Cessna. I used it to bid jobs in Colorado, Kansas, Nebraska and Wyoming.

Berniece's dad had an appendicitis attack while on a cruise to Alaska. The tour group had to go on without him because he got sick and had to go to the hospital. Berniece and I flew up to bring him and Lorane back home. When we got to the hospital, Harlan reached out, grabbed my hand and thanked me for coming to Alaska to get them. I was glad to do that. We brought them to our house in Lakewood, then Berniece's brother, Richard, and a friend, Bob Waldman, flew Richard's plane out and one of them drove them back in Harlan's car to Oakley.

For a while, almost every Saturday I got together with a group of fifteen or twenty pilots at a church in East Denver. (Berniece enjoyed shopping on those Saturdays while I was gone.) The guys and I would have coffee and devotions, decide where we were going to fly that day, then go to the airport, get in our planes and take off. We liked flying around in Colorado and Kansas. Some of us wanted to fly our own planes, and others just wanted to ride along. We'd fly somewhere and get what we called a "$25 hamburger." (That's what the pilot got for taking his plane. We'd ride with each other, and the passengers would kick in to buy lunch for the pilot.)

One time we flew thirteen airplanes to Dodge City. We had a "flying club" if you want to call it that. Some of us were ex-military, and some were not. There were one or two that were wealthy, and there were some that hardly had enough money to buy the fuel for their planes.

THIRTY ONE
WYCLIFFE BIBLE TRANSLATORS

Steve Ottaviano, who was a JAARS (Jungle Aviation and Radio Services)[1] missionary pilot serving in Peru, came to our church and wondered if we would help with his support. We voted unanimously that we would. That was the start of our involvement with Wycliffe Bible Translators and JAARS. The first time I met Steve was when he came to one of our men's meetings with the pilots. He was just finishing his pilot's training.

One night at church Jerry, one of the pilots in our flying group, mentioned that we should buy a new plane for the Wycliffe missionaries in South America. He did all the paperwork to buy a new Cessna. After we bought the plane, we pilots had a meeting and decided that we needed to pray and dedicate the plane to God for His use in the jungles of South America. We set a date on a Saturday morning for the dedication, and there were about 200 people who came to the East Colfax Airport.

A young ham radio operator came with a shortwave radio system, which he set up so we could talk to a missionary in Peru. The noise from Peru was so great that we could hardly make out anything the missionary was saying. The radio operator turned the volume down, and Jerry asked if anybody had a special request. Jerry was going to deliver the plane to South America, and we prayed for him to have safety on his way there and back.

We had a preacher there at the airport, and as we held hands and formed a circle around that plane, we asked that it be used totally for God's work on the mission field in South America. The guy turned the volume back up on the short-wave radio, and there was not one bit of static or noise. We heard the missionary in South America very clearly! When the last man finished praying, at that very minute, the static came over that shortwave radio again, and we couldn't hear a thing. God blessed so we could dedicate that plane to the Lord and communicate with the missionary. We left there with happy hearts!

Jerry flew the plane to Peru to be used by the missionaries who went up the Amazon River. When one of the missionaries came home, he told us that it had previously taken him two weeks to get out to a certain tribe in the jungle, but with the plane, it took only two hours and ten minutes. He was so grateful for the plane.

Some of those natives accepted Jesus Christ as their Savior. Later, a missionary brought two or three of them to the church on the east side of Denver to share their testimonies. Somebody asked them, "Why didn't you kill the missionary when he was walking across the country?" He said, "We had decided we would kill him, but we didn't because of that great big, tall guy that was standing beside him. He was taller than everybody else, and we turned and ran." There was no man with that missionary! God had protected him supernaturally and had put someone in their path that only they could see. Those are the things that are real to me.

THIRTY TWO
MISSION TRIP TO SOUTH AMERICA

When we were closing our Bland Electric company, Wycliffe Bible Translators asked Berniece and me if we would go to South America to put in some electricity at a new camp. This was the start of my love for mission work and was brought together with my love for flying. Berniece and I both felt God's call to go to Peru.

We were all set to go, and they called me the day before we were to leave and said, "Well, we're not ready. You'll have to wait a week." I didn't like that very much. This old Irish temper of mine flared, and I told them I couldn't make it in a week and hung up. Berniece said, "Mr. Bland, you made a mistake."

It wasn't very long before I got another call wanting me to do almost the same job in a different camp. I didn't hesitate. I said, "We'll go." We packed up, flew out of Denver and landed in Lima, Peru.

When we got down there, Berniece immediately went to work in the office. I had to wait a while for the materials to arrive for the job Wycliffe wanted me to do. We went to three different places for about a week each.

Food for the Hungry is an organization out of Arizona. They were down in Peru and were working on putting in a water well for the people that lived in the desert. One day I was standing in the courtyard in Lima, and the missionary who oversaw their work came over, put his arm around me and said, "Would you come up to the desert and put in a well for us?" (Bob Lewallen and I used to do wells.) I said, "We're down here for Wycliffe, and I don't think they want us to leave." One of the Wycliffe workers heard me and said, "You have to wait for this stuff anyway, so why don't you go and do the work for them in the meantime?" I said, "It's up to you because I'm assigned to you." It was agreed that I would go.

Berniece went with me, and we were taken up to the northern part of Peru by plane. When we got there, Berniece was given an English-speaking maid to help her.

I was loaded up in a crazy old junk car and taken out to a site where they were going to put in the water well. When we got to the site, there was a big cement block wall enclosure, and right in the middle was a casing for the well. It was made of scrap iron and angle iron.

There was a young man there from California who had given his life to serve the Lord in South America. He had a welder. With a stick, I drew a windmill tower on the sand floor of the enclosure. I said, "Can you figure out what I'm doing?" He said, "Yeah." I told him, "I want a 30-foot tower welded together out of these angle irons. This is what we're going to use to put the pipe down the well." He got busy, but I didn't watch him because I knew I didn't need to. He made the tower shaped like a Kansas windmill.

The next day, we went back and started putting 320 feet of 1¼ inch galvanized water pipe down that well. We used his Japanese-made pickup, with a wench on the front, to let the pipe down into the well. We'd let down a section and then we'd screw the two pipes together and hold them with a rope. Each section was twenty feet long, and we would tape the electric wire to them as we put them down. I tried to get the workers to make me a pipe dog* and even drew a picture of one, but I couldn't get them to understand what that was.

We used a section of that pipe to make a barrier so the people wouldn't come into where we were working. When we got down close to 320 feet and had put on the last piece of pipe, I said to the guy from California, "Buddy, hook that up and we'll see what we've got." We opened the gate to let in the hundreds of natives waiting out there with buckets.

Sinbad, my Chinese interpreter, and all the people were watching the end of the pipe, but nothing happened. I walked over, covered it with my hand, and I could feel compression. I came back and told Sinbad, "It's coming." Suddenly rusty water came pouring out! The people were so excited! They got their buckets and started catching water. Sinbad was glad to see that water too. I told him, "Tell them to wait, and it will clear up." He said, "I already did." He went again and talked to them, came back and said, "They don't think it's gonna last that long." Well, it did clear up. Two little white-haired old men came up to us, and they were crying. They told Sinbad they wanted to shake the

---

* A pipe dog is a tool used for lifting and setting pipes.[1]

hand of the American who came to South America and gave them drinking water. I said, "I'm not the one who did that. I'm just doing the work. The Lord Jesus Himself gave you this water."

The women came with whatever buckets they had. They didn't push, shove or holler. They came one at a time, filled their buckets with clear water and carried it out. More came all the time. I found out later that there were about 700 people living in that desert who hadn't had a drop of water to drink without walking many miles for it. We got water to them, and it was a jubilee time because they were so elated to have water come out of a pipe in their back yard. I asked a guy from Food for the Hungry to keep me informed if that well stayed good or dried up, but I thought it was going to stay.

The next job was at Yarinacocha on the Amazon River. We hadn't planned to go there, but I got a call from California asking us if we would, and I knew better than to say no, so we went. Berniece's job was to teach school, and I was to hook up a great big, used generator that had been donated to Wycliffe. They didn't have anybody to put in the wiring, so I volunteered. They flew us over the Andes Mountains, and we landed in Yarinacocha in east central Peru. We debarked there and rode a truck out to the site of the village. When I got there, none of the guys knew how to wire that generator. All they did was dig a ditch and put a wire in it, so I put in underground cable and a big overload switch for the generator that was to supply electricity for that area of Peru. I thought they wanted somebody to splice a big wire, and I said, "I'm not a lineman. I'm an inside wireman."

They had four linemen from Tennessee that did the big stuff, then all I had to do was put in the control cable and that kind of work. It was a blessing to me and a blessing for them too that we could work together to get the job done.

After working on that for a while, I rented a sea plane from JAARS, and Berniece and I took a little time to go to a village where Wycliffe had translated the Bible into the natives' own language. After we landed, some of the kids stood in the water and held two canoes together so we could get out of the plane without getting our feet wet. That was very kind of them.

We wanted to go to their church. The building was several feet off the ground to keep the animals from coming in. While we were there, the little kids sang songs to us which they had learned in English. It was a melody to my heart!

We flew back to the village at Yarinacocha, landing on the Ucayali River. We finished the job and got the generator running. It was an old timer, but the village now had its own electricity, and Wycliffe could plug in their computers to translate the Bible into the language of the natives so they could learn about Jesus Christ.

In Lima, all the guys who came down there without a spouse had to sleep in a dormitory. Because we were a married couple, Berniece and I had a room of our own at the Lima House which was built for missionaries and volunteers who were there to help in some way.

While we were there, Berniece and I had a chance to sit down and talk with Steve Ottaviano. He and I became friends, and we still stay in contact. I am thankful for his friendship. He and his wife continue to serve the Lord in

Papua New Guinea as of this writing.

One time as we were sitting there after our meal at the Lima House, about eight or ten guys were telling Navy stories. Many of the pilots that worked for JAARS were old Navy pilots like me. They were from World War II and had already retired from their jobs. They gave their lives to the Lord and went to the mission field to serve Him by flying planes that had been given to Wycliffe.

I got up from the table to look at the books that were there and pulled out the book, *Into the Glory*. As I was thinking, something told me, "I know these guys." I said to them, "You guys are in the book." One of them asked, "What do you mean?" I said, "You're in Jamie Buckingham's book, *Into the Glory*, about the Jungle Aviation and Radio Services ministry." They looked at me, and one of them commented, "Yeah, I guess so." Berniece and I talked to them, and I told them, "I've got this book, and I really like it." They said, "Well, we don't read the books, we just go out and do the work." They had lots of stories to tell! I enjoyed our time together.

Into the Glory chronicles the lives and ministries of the JAARS pilots who flew for Wycliffe Bible Translators. Steve Ottaviano was one of those pilots mentioned in the book.

These are rugged people who have heard the call of Christ to come away from the glory of the crowds and comfortable living to serve naked aborigines and headhunters whose languages have never been committed to writing. Sometimes their only thanks is a brandished spear. But sometimes, far above the clouds, they do enjoy the momentary glory of looking down at the shadow their little crafts cast on the cloud-tops. Around that shadow a peculiar dispersion of the sun's rays creates a corona of light. Pilots have long called that corona "the glory" and when they finally have to descend beneath the clouds, they fly "into the glory." At the moment the plane and shadow converge at the cloud there is a virtual explosion of light. And in a special sense for the pilots of JAARS they do fly into the glory — the glory of serving the least of all the peoples of the earth in obedience to Jesus Christ.[2]

One incident we saw of God's power happened one morning before breakfast. While we were sitting there talking to the JAARS pilots, the lady who cooked and served our meals said we couldn't eat until we prayed specifically for a pilot who was going in to rescue people who had been taken captive by The Shining Path* drug runners.

The lady got on the radio later and found out how God had protected the pilot and those who were with him. The pilot had made four trips back and forth to pick up native pastors, missionaries and translators. When the plane flew in, the captives would come running out of the jungle to the dirt runway to be picked up. He would take them downriver and come back to get more people. When they landed, the pilot would have to get out to turn the plane around by hand because the runway wasn't wide enough to turn it around while maneuvering it from inside the plane. The drug runners never heard the plane approach or take off, and all the captives were rescued safely. That's how God worked in answer to our prayers!

Another time when we were in the dining room of the

---

* The Shining Path was the official Communist Party of Peru and a recognized guerilla group.[3]

Lima House, the guys were talking about the cattle that had been flown down there. A rancher from South Texas got saved then went to Peru on a mission trip. He said, "What this place needs is a bunch of Brahmas." He made the arrangements to load them up, and several of his cattle were flown to the terminal in South America. Berniece and I saw some of those Brahma cattle walking all around in one of the villages we visited. As far as I know, they were still there producing babies and feeding the people.

THIRTY THREE
HOME AGAIN

When Berniece and I finished our time in Peru, the people from Food for the Hungry tried to get us to move down there to work on the program of teaching those people a trade, but I declined.

We came home, and all three of our kids met us at Stapleton Airport. I talked to them about their mother and me becoming missionaries. They wanted us to do it, and we tried.

As soon as we got back, Wycliffe wanted me to go to the Philippines to hook up a big generator at a boarding school for missionary kids who came there from different areas of the South Pacific. They'd stay there during the school year, then go back home.

There was a disgruntled man who had been to the Philippines who said, "Well, he can't be a Wycliffe missionary because he hasn't been to Bible School." I asked him why that was a problem. He said, "What if one of those people who can't speak English asks you whose sins it was that Jesus died for. Could you tell them?" I said, "Tell 'em? I've been doing that for twenty years." He told me, "Yeah, but not in their language." I said, "I don't care what language it's in."

Wycliffe said I couldn't do it. We had our things ready, but I guess we got discouraged and decided not to go. We had planned to move to Orange County, California, and get an apartment there at the center for Wycliffe Bible Translators. I was going to go by myself to the Philippines to hook up that generator for the school, but it didn't happen. I guess God didn't want me there because I didn't know how to tell them about Him in their language. We had $7,000 given to us from our church. I had to go tell the treasurers to give it back to the church, and that's what they did. I like Food for the Hungry and Wycliffe Bible Translators, but I didn't have any Bible School training. Nevertheless, it was a good time in our lives. I look back on that era and am thankful for it. I feel blessed.

———————

One Sunday, I was handed a book, *Through Gates of Splendor*, about five missionaries who went to South America to witness to Indian tribes in Ecuador. One of those couples was Jim and Elisabeth Elliot. I still have the book.

In the 1950's, Jim and four other missionaries were in a Piper Cub trying to make contact with the Auca Indians. Their purpose was to tell them the message of Jesus Christ and reach them for the Lord. The contact was going well, but then the Aucas attacked them, killed all five men and destroyed the plane.

Elisabeth took her young daughter, Valerie, and went back to live with those same Aucas who had killed her husband. She was able to forgive them, and lead many of them to Christ. That was how God worked in her life and in theirs.

She later came to our church in Lakewood and brought some of the Aucas with her. We got to meet them in their native dress. They looked pretty scary! They said they were part of the group that had killed Jim Elliott and the four other missionaries in Ecuador. One of them admitted that he was the one who did it. What an example of God's redemption, healing and reconciliation!

THIRTY FOUR
THE MOTHER I NEVER KNEW

Sometime after I had re-connected with my Shugart siblings, I wanted to know about and try to find my mother, Cora Shugart. For a long time, when I would ask them where she was, they would look at each other in a kinda funny way, but all I could get them to say was, "Oh, she's a very nice woman." I never knew why they didn't want to talk to me about her. They finally told me that she was living with her sister, Phoebie Frost, in Topeka.

I learned that Phoebie's son, Gerald, worked for the Topeka Police Department. He went by the nickname "Frosty." Berniece and I contacted the Police Department and asked if I could speak to Frosty. When he answered the phone, I said, "You don't know me, but I think you know my mother, Cora Anna (Hunt) Shugart." He said, "Yes, I know exactly who you are." He knew that I was her son. We met him and his wife in a restaurant in Topeka. He told me, "She lived with us, and I took care of her after she got hit." I asked him, "Hit. What do you mean?" He told me that Walter hit her on the head with a hammer. He said she had seizures ever since that time.

He went on to say that she would wander around on the streets, and many times he would have to go get her. He'd ask her, "Aunt Cora, what are you doing out here?" She'd say, "I'm looking for Donnie." She had asked where I was and was told that I had died. She didn't believe that, and she continually looked for me. Her health got worse, and I think her heart was broken that she didn't ever find me. I've always wished I could have known her.

THIRTY FIVE
50TH WEDDING ANNIVERSARY

Berniece and I went back to Whidbey Island for our 50th wedding anniversary. It was so special! We had a good time there. We always said we had a five-month honeymoon, and we did. I have a newspaper article that says:

They say you can never go home again, but Mr. and Mrs. Don Bland proved that's not right, because they came to Whidbey Island, Washington, for their 50-year anniversary.

"SEA DREAM LODGE REMEMBERED"

They drove from Kansas to see the place they had once called home but had not seen for 50 years. All the way to Coupeville, Don and Berniece Bland wondered if the little cottage could possibly still be there next to the park and behind Maude Fullington's home on the bluff above the cove. They were afraid it would be gone; that perhaps they would be unable to recognize what had once meant so much to them both.

Don had grown up in an orphanage, alone. [sic] When he was old enough [sic] he joined the Navy and married his

High School Sweetheart. Ordered to Whidbey Island, he found the Sea Dream Lodge, rented it from Maude Fullington for $50.00 a month, and brought his bride west. During the trip he kept telling her they would have to live in a tent, figuring she would be so relieved to find an actual house at the end of their journey that she wouldn't be disappointed by its size and lack of conveniences. He guessed right. Sea Dream Lodge had been built by Judge Lester Sill sometime after the turn of the 20th century. Constructed of logs branches and rocks, it was un-usual and charming with two small bedrooms and bathroom, a living room with a tiny dining area, built close to Coveland Street and facing the town park. It's [sic] mullioned windows were topped by a row of glass photographic plates, their images of sailing ships fading away over time. Rocks and shards and bits of glass were embedded in the cemented walls, and panes of stained glass were on either side of the front door.

Though the cottage had only a woodstove to cook on, and a kerosene heater and fireplace were the sole sources of heat, the young couple spent the first five months of their married life quite contentedly. Don arranged with his landlady that he would repair the cottage for a deduction in the rent. One day Maude returned from Seattle with a salvaged set of windows to replace the original windows with mullions made of branches, since the wood was disintegrating, and the panes rattled in the wind. During the process a part of the front rock wall collapsed — to the young couple's horror — and they quickly mortared it back up.

Maude Fullington was a memorable landlady. She told the young couple stories about how Rudolph Valentino, among other theatrical folk, would sail up from Hollywood and into

Penn Cove, where he would tie up at the Fullington Dock and then stay for days in Maude's atmospheric old house. She clearly favored Valentino over all the others which would come as no surprise, according to the Blands. Don and Berniece remember Maude gardening in black shorts — unusual attire for ladies at the time and wearing orange cotton stockings to keep the sun off her legs. Dragging bull kelp up from the beach, Maude would lay it out under the rosebushes and trail it through her garden, much to the amusement of her renters.

The Blands arrived in Coupeville last month to find that though their cottage was gone and the Fullington House in its place, everything still looked comfortingly familiar. They wandered hand in hand through the garden, stopping on the lawn where their bedroom once stood."

"Will you take our picture?" Don asked. "This is where our first son got his start." With that he bent over his wife of exactly fifty years, surrounded by the remembered walls of a honeymoon long past and kissed her.

Sea Dream Lodge is only a dream now. It was reduced to rubble when the Fullington House had to be moved farther from the bluff. But one midsummer afternoon it was possible to imagine its walls were still here, restored by cherished memory.

Thomas Wolffe wrote that we can never go home again. Sometimes we can.

By Sally Hayton Keeva[1]

I like to repeat the saying, "Make good memories because they're roses in the wintertime." That's what you live on when you're older.

THIRTY SIX
RETIREMENT IN KANSAS

Berniece and I wanted to retire somewhere away from Denver. We considered several places and decided to buy forty acres of property about eight miles northwest of McPherson. We wanted to be close to Donnie and his family.

I sold my airplane so we could buy a fifth-wheel trailer and travel. Berniece enjoyed that. We lived in the trailer while we built a shop on the property. After the shop was finished, we parked the trailer inside and continued to live in it as we began building the house. I used the same house plans that Berniece liked from a house I had wired in Denver.

Donnie helped me build, and I hired some other guys to help too. One of them was another Don. We said I was Don 1, Donnie was Don 2, and he was Don 3. Another young man who helped was Cameron Koster, the grandson of Lucille Bruns, a friend from Winona.

When we were finished, Berniece and I stood out front, and she said to me, "Mr. Bland, you sure built me an awfully nice house!" Our goal was to use the house and property for the glory of the Lord. We planned to make it a place where missionaries could come and stay while they were home on furlough or in the area for other reasons.

We had many wonderful years together living in our home in the country. Our house is less than fifty miles from Dillon, Kansas, where I was born.

In 2007, Berniece had to go into the hospital for heart surgery. After having complications, the Lord took her home to be with Him on February 19, 2007. She was the "air beneath my wings." Always by my side, she supported me throughout our years together. She was a prayer warrior, and I know that God worked in our lives because of her faithful prayers. I have missed her so much and have been very lonely living without her. I am grateful to God that we will see each other again and will be together for eternity. Next to meeting my Lord and Savior Jesus Christ, she is the one my heart longs to see again!

THIRTY SEVEN
UNEXPECTED HONORS

An event for which I will always be grateful was the Kansas Honor Flight to Washington, D.C. Because of donations to the program, veterans were able to go at no charge. What a blessing!

I'm thankful Donnie went with me as my "guardian." He pushed me in a wheelchair because there was too much walking for me to be able to see everything.

As we got off the plane in Chicago at O'Hare Airport, there were two moving sidewalks. When the people on those sidewalks looked up and saw us, they stepped off and started clapping. I know it wasn't planned. I thought, "Why are they clapping? I didn't do anything." I talked to the lady in charge and said to her, "I never did anything." She said, "You raised your right hand, didn't you?" She asked how long I was in the Navy. I said, "Five years." She said, "Most of the guys come home by the time their fourth year's up. You're just as important as anyone. You served your time, so enjoy!" Every place we went, the people stopped to honor us.

The World War II Memorial was a special place. There

was a lady who had her grandson with her, and she said he wanted to talk to me. He said, "I want to thank you for your service." The lady looked at me and winked. I told him that he had a good Dad who taught him to be thankful. I asked the lady if the boy's grandpa had been in the military. She said, "Yes, but he's dead now." I looked at him and said, "Always remember that your grandpa was very important to our country!" Times like that are what I treasure!

We got over to the Mall, and there was a lady dressed up like they did in the 1940's. She came over to me and said, "Sailor, you want to dance? Do you know the Lindy Hop?" I said, "Yeah, but I can't do it in this chair." She said, "That's ok, we're going to dance the Lindy Hop, and I'm going to dance it around the wheelchair." She did!

It was very special to me that we saw our Senator, Jerry Moran, and Representative, Tim Huelskamp. They both came down and gave talks to our group.

The woman who got me on the flight said, "There's somebody else here that you might want to talk to. He's not on the program." I said, "Who is it?" She said, "Go around the curve, and you'll see him sitting there." It was Bob Dole. I walked over, and he said, "I want to thank you for serving." I told him, "Bob, I want to thank you for getting the VA Center in Wichita straightened out." I sat beside him, and we talked. I said to him, "You don't know me, but I know you. When you were running for the House, I was living out by Winona, and we came to the fair in Oakley. You were shaking everybody's hands and asking them for their vote. I told you I'd give you mine. Two years later, you came back with your entourage with you. I walked up to you and said, "My name is…" You said, "I know who you are. You're Don Bland." (I was amazed that he remembered my name after two years.) Somebody said, "That's the way he is. He knows everybody's name." While I was talking to him, he asked, "Do you know Judge Spencer?" I said, "You're talking about Corwin Spencer, aren't you? He did my taxes for a number of years." He said, "Good man, good man!" It was an honor for me to see him because he was a veteran too and had been crippled during the war. People thought he was putting on, but he wasn't. He always carried a pencil or pen in his injured right hand so nobody would try to shake it because it hurt.

There was one black guy on the flight with us who had been a Master Sergeant in the Army. Here came a black lady, and she had a little boy with her. The guy was somewhere else in the line. She asked, "Can I talk to you?" I said, "Yes." She told me that her grandpa was on the flight with me. I said, "Yes, I ate supper with him last night. He's very interesting!" She said, "I've got my son here with me. Would you talk to him?" I said, "Sure." Of course, we were all wearing Honor Flight tee shirts and hats. The little boy had a card that he had written by himself. His writing was not straight. It said, "Thank you for serving." I told him, "Well, that's nice, and I thank you. You know, I think I ate supper with your great grandpa last night. You need to respect him because he is a good guy and quite a wonderful man! He served his country." I built him up as much as I could for that little guy. The little boy's eyes got bigger and bigger, and he thanked me again for serving. His mom turned to me and thanked me.

The Korean War Memorial was spooky. In Korea, everyone wore ponchos because it rained there so much of the time. The statues are so intricate that I could look at them and tell what rifle they were carrying.

We had a good night. We saw more things the next day and then got back on our flight and came home through Chicago. We were gone for only 48 hours.

───────────

I was honored to be included in the June 2022 annual celebration of D-Day at the Eisenhower Presidential Library and Museum in Abilene. There were four of us veterans from the World War II and Korean War time periods who were asked to talk to people who would come by our tables and want to know about our military experiences. The day was one to remember! We were treated like royalty! There were even golf carts to take us from place to place.

In the evening, we were seated right up front for the Symphony at Sunset Concert. We were recognized for our service to our country. They played the "Armed Forces Medley." I was proud to stand and salute when they came to "Anchors Aweigh." That sure brought back memories!

One of the highlights of the day was when President Eisenhower's granddaughter and his great-grandson came by to speak to each one of us individually. President Eisenhower was a great president, and it was an honor to be greeted by some of his family.

THIRTY EIGHT
A WONDERFUL LIFE

Music has always been very important to me. As I look back over the years, this song pretty much sums up what I'd like to say about what God has done in my life. Even though there are parts I would love to erase, through it all, I've had a wonderful life.

Carroll Roberson is one of my favorite gospel singers and songwriters. It is with permission that I end my story with one of my favorite songs written by him. I've listened to it many times during these last several lonely months, and the words speak of what's in my heart.

"A WONDERFUL LIFE"
(Song by Carroll Roberson, 1996)
Used by Permission

I've had a wonderful life.
The Lord's been so good to me.
I've had a wonderful life,
If tomorrow I never see.

If I had no more blessings in store,
I'd never ask or wonder why.
If I died today, I could honestly say,
I've had a wonderful life.

I've had some good times,
I've seen the bad,
But thanks to Jesus my heart's not sad.
I'm happy today.

Even though I have some regrets,
There's one thing I'll never forget,
Jesus stood by my side all of the way.

I've had a wonderful life.
The Lord's been so good to me.
I've had a wonderful life,
If tomorrow I never see.

If I had no more blessings in store,
I'd never ask or wonder why.
If I died today, I could honestly say,
I've had a wonderful life.
(I've had a wonderful life.
The Lord's been so good to me.)

I've had a wonderful life,
If tomorrow I never see.
If I had no more blessings in store,
I'd never ask or wonder why.

If I died today, I could honestly say,
I've had a wonderful life.

If I had no more blessings in store,
I'd never ask or wonder why.
If I died today, I could honestly say,
I've had a wonderful life.

I've had a wonderful life.
I've had a wonderful life.[1]

Although I would have written my life story in a different way, God allowed all of these events to come to me through His hands. I'm thankful that He had His hand of protection on me even in times of tremendous pain. I'm thankful for the opportunities He has given me to tell others of His love and salvation. May all the glory and praise be given to our Lord and Savior, Jesus Christ! If there's any good to be seen, it's because of Him.

May you choose to surrender your life to Him and let Him write your story. God sums it up this way, "For My thoughts are not your thoughts, neither are your ways My ways, declares the LORD. For as the heavens are higher than the earth, so are My ways higher than your ways, and My thoughts than your thoughts" (Isaiah 55:9 KJV). As I look back on my life, I have to say, thank You, Lord Jesus! It's because of You and only through You that I've had a wonderful life.

EPILOGUE

Uncle Don went to be with our Lord and Savior on February 1, 2023. He is now in his eternal home with his Heavenly Father and his dear Berniece. (The date of her death was February 19, 2007. His burial took place February 20, which would have been their 72nd wedding anniversary.)

It was his prayer that his story would be a way to reach others with the gospel of Christ. While on earth, he retold it many, many times. It is now in print for you to read.

If he was still here, he would want to know your spiritual condition. The cry of his heart was to see that others knew the way to heaven and how you too could have a saving faith in Jesus Christ, the only mediator between God and man.

Uncle Don would have loved to share these Bible verses with you:

"For God so loved the world, that He gave His only begotten Son, that whoever believes in Him should not perish, but have eternal life" (John 3:16).

"As it is written, there is none righteous, not even one;" (Romans 3:10).

"For all have sinned and fall short of the glory of God,"

(Romans 3:23).

"But God demonstrated His own love toward us, in that while we were yet sinners, Christ died for us" (Romans 5:8).

"For the wages of sin is death, but the free gift of God is eternal life in Christ Jesus our Lord" (Romans 6:23).

"That if you confess with your mouth Jesus as Lord, and believe in your heart that God raised Him from the dead, you shall be saved; for with the heart man believes, resulting in righteousness, and with the mouth he confesses, resulting in salvation" (Romans 10:9–10).

"For whoever will call upon the name of the Lord will be saved" (Romans 10:13).

Thank you, Lord, for Uncle Don's life. Thank you that You used him to have such an impact in my life as he shared his faith in You. I look forward to being together with him again as we worship at Your feet!

What a privilege it has been to work with him on his book. For me, what started out as answering Your call from James 1:27 to visit him, (an orphan and a widower), became one of the greatest blessings of my life! My hope and intent was to bring joy to his heart and to help him realize how loved and valued he was.

Thank You for Your wisdom and help in bringing this book to completion. May Your Name be glorified through his incredible story!

Barbara Zimmerman

NOTES

Foreword

1. USLegal, "Orphan Law and Legal Definition," Accessed November 6, 2023, https://definitions.uslegal.com/o/orphan/.

One

1. District Court of Dickinson County, Kansas, "In the Interest of Donald Shugart, a minor under the age of 18 years," Case No. 3388, May 1, 1979, private collection.
2. Kansas Children's Home and Service League, Topeka, Kansas, Donald Earl Shugart Case Records, Case No. 4151, private collection.
3. Juvenile Court of the State of Kansas, Dickinson County, "Final Order for Dependent and Neglected Child," September 14, 1932, private collection.
4. Kansas Children's Home and Service League, Shugart Case Supplementary History, Case No. 4151, September 17, 1932–November 30, 1932, private collection.

Two

1. Kansas Children's Home and Service League, Donald Earl Shugart, Case No. 4151, January 6, 1933–May 1, 1933, private collection.

Three

1. Kansas Historical Society, "Jackrabbit Drives," March 2009, accessed November 6, 2023, https://www.kshs.org/kansapedia/jackabbit-drives/12097.

Four

1. Kansas Children's Home and Service League, Donald Earl Shugart Case No. 4151, Report of Visit to Child, November 10, 1937, private collection.
2. Ibid., Notes from case worker, September 12, 1938, May 20, 1940, private collection.
3. Ibid., July 28, 1941.

Five

1. Max Moxley, "Rice County History…Then and Now," accessed November 6, 2023, https://sterling.digitalsckls.info/history-of-sterling.
2. Kansas Children's Home and Service League, Donald Earl Shugart Case No. 4151, Report of Visit to Child, May 28, 1940, July 28, 1941, private collection.
3. Ibid., December 1941, private collection.

Six

1. Kansas Children's Home and Service League, April 22, 1942, private collection.
2. Voice of America, "American History: US Declares War on Japan, Germany and Italy," accessed November 8, 2023, https://www.51voa.com/VOA_Special_English/American-History-The-United-States-Declares-War-First-on-Japan-Then-Germany-and-Italy--41989.html.
3. Kansas Children's Home and Service League, __-10-1941, 12, private collection.
4. Ibid., April 22, 1942, 15.

Eight

1. Kansas Children's Home and Service League, May 18, 1942, October 2, 1942, 16, private collection.
2. Amy Bickel, Kansas-Agland, "'Betrayed by a Fingerprint' Kansas' Fleagle Gang," The Hutchinson News (Hutchinson, Kansas), January 28, 2016, accessed November 8, 2023, https://www.hutchnews.com > local "Betrayed by a Fingerprint" Kansas' Fleagle Gang.

Ten

1. Kansas Children's Home and Service League, May 24, 1943, July 1, 1943, 17–19, private collection.
2. Ibid., October 28, 1943, 20.
3. Ibid., 21–23.
4. Probate Court of Gove County, Kansas, "In the Matter of the Petition of Letia O. Bland, a widow to adopt Donald Earl, A Minor Child," Case No. 1336, March 24, 1944, private collection.
5. Kansas Children's Home and Service League, Transfer Summary, March 30, 1944, October 31, 1944, January 18, 1945, 23–32, private collection.
6. Wikipedia, "Andrew Drumm Institute," October 30, 2023, accessed November 6, 2023, https://en.wikipedia.org/wiki/Andrew_Drumm_Institute.
7. Kansas Children's Home and Service League, February 16–17, 1945, 32–34, private collection.
8. Ibid., Transfer Summary, March 3, 1945, 34–36, private collection.
9. Probate Court of Gove County, Kansas, Application to dismiss adoption proceedings, Case No. 1336, March 6, 1945, private collection.
10. Benj. J. Hegler, Kansas Children's Home and Service League, letter to Jesse I. Linder, Attorney at Law, March 5, 1945, private collection.
11. Kansas Children's Home and Service League, Transfer Case to Topeka, March 8, 1945, 36–38, private collection.

Eleven

1. Kansas Children's Home and Service League, Transfer Case to Topeka, March 8, 1945, 38–39, private collection.

Twelve

1. Miss Marjorie Foulke, Acting State Case Supervisor, Kansas Children's Home and Service League, letter to Mr. Clifford Bland, July 12, 1945, private collection.
2. Mrs. Leila N. Myers, Case Supervisor, Topeka, Kansas Children's Home and Service League, letter to Mr. Benj. F. Hegler, July 19, 1945, private collection.

Thirteen

1. Find A Grave (http://www.findagrave.com: accessed November 8, 2023), Memorial ID 73224167, Clifford James Bland (1896–1945) Created by Barb Werner, Added: July 11, 2011, Gove Cemetery, Gove, Gove County, Kansas, USA, https://www.findagrave.com/memorial/73224167/clifford-james-bland.

Fifteen

1. Kansas Children's Home and Service League, September 24, 1946, November 1, 1946, 39, private collection.

Sixteen

1. Wikipedia, "City of St. Louis (train)," September 4, 2023, accessed November 6, 2023, https://en.wikipedia.org/wiki/City_of_St._Louis_(train).
2. Wikipedia, "Naval Air Technical Training Center Ward Island," July 14, 2023, accessed November 6, 2023, https://en.wikipedia.org/wiki/Naval_Air_Technical_Training_Center_Ward_Island.

Seventeen

1. Naval History and Heritage Command, "Higgins Boats," July 22, 2021, accessed November 6, 2023, https://www.history.navy.mil Higgins Boats – Naval History and Heritage Command.
2. Mrs. Dora A. Payne, Executive Secretary and Miss Florence Walker, Home Service Worker, letter to Kansas Children's Home and Service

League, RE: Marion Walter Shugart, February 12, 1945, private collection.

Nineteen

1. Wikipedia, "Lockheed P-2 Neptune," November 3, 2023, accessed November 6, 2023, https://en.wikipedia.org/wiki/Lockheed_P-2_Neptune.
2. David Wilma, "Sand Point Naval Air Station: 1920–1970," HistoryLink.org Essay 2249, accessed November 6, 2023, April 3, 2000, https://www.historylink.org/file/2249.

Twenty

1. National WWII Museum, "'Angels of Okinawa,'": The F4U Corsair, May 3, 2020, accessed November 6, 2023, https://www.nationalww2museum.org "Angels of Okinawa".
2. Wikipedia, "Charles Lindbergh." November 3, 2023, accessed November 6, 2023, https://en.wikipedia.org/wiki/Charles_Lindbergh.

Twenty Three

1. Wikipedia, "Orphan Train," July 13,2024, accessed July 21, 2024, https://en.wikipedia.org/wiki/Orphan_Train.
2. Martha Nelson Vogt, and Christina Vogt, *Searching for Home*, (Hillsboro, Kansas: Triumph Press), 1995.

Twenty Seven

1. Steve Adams, Embracing Brokenness Ministries, "The Bummer Lamb," accessed November 8, 2023, https://embracingbrokenness.org/2019/12/the-bummer-lamb/.

Twenty Eight

1. Mrs. Emily D.Wilson, "I Will Pilot Thee," 1927.

Thirty

1. Michael Robert Patterson, "'High Flight,'" November 3, 2023, accessed November 6, 2023, https://www.arlingtoncemetery.net/highflig.htm.

Thirty One

1. Wikipedia, "JAARS," November 1, 2023, accessed November 6, 2023, https://en.m.wikipedia.org JAARS.

Thirty Two

1. America West Drilling Company, Pipe Dogs lifting and setting tools, accessed November 8, 2023, https://americawestdrillingsupply.com/pipe-dogs-pipe-lifting-and-setting/.
2. Jamie Buckingham, *Into the Glory*, (Plainfield, New Jersey: Logos International), 1974, Excerpt from front cover.
3. Wikipedia, "Shining Path," June 11, 2024, accessed July 21, 2024, https://en.wikipedia.org/wiki/Shining_Path.

Thirty Five

1. Sally Hayton Keeva, "Sea Dream Lodge Remembered," private collection.

Thirty Eight

1. Carroll Roberson, "A Wonderful Life," 1996.

BIBLIOGRAPHY

Sources

Adams, Steve. Embracing Brokenness Ministries. "The Bummer Lamb." accessed November 8, 2023. https://embracingbrokenness.org/2019/12/the-bummer-lamb/.

Buckingham, Jamie. *Into the Glory*. (Plainfield, New Jersey: Logos International, 1974), Excerpt from front cover.

District Court of Dickinson County, Kansas. "In the Interest of Donald Shugart, a minor under the age of 18 years." Case No. 3388. May 1, 1979.

Find A Grave (http://www.findagrave.com: accessed November 8, 2023). Memorial ID 73224167. Clifford James Bland (1896–1945). Created by Barb Werner. Added: July 11, 2011. Gove Cemetery. Gove, Gove County, Kansas, USA. https://www.findagrave.com/memorial/73224167/clifford-james-bland.

Kansas Children's Home and Service League. Topeka, Kansas. Shugart Case. Donald Earl Shugart Case. Case numbers 4151, 1336 and 3388. September 14, 1932–May 1, 1979.

Keeva, Sally Hayton. "Sea Dream Lodge Remembered." private collection.

Patterson, Michael Robert. "'High Flight.'" November 3, 2023. accessed November 6, 2023. https://www.arlingtoncemetery.net/highflig.htm.

Payne, Mrs. Dora A., Executive Secretary and Miss Florence Walker, Home Service Worker, letter to Kansas Children's Home and Service League, RE: Marion Walter Shugart, February 12, 1945.

Probate Court of Gove County, Kansas. "Application to dismiss adoption proceedings." Case No. 1336. March 6, 1945.

Probate Court of Gove County, Kansas. "In the Matter of the Petition of Letia O. Bland, a Widow to adopt Donald Earl, A Minor Child." Case No. 1336. March 24, 1944.

Roberson, Carroll. "A Wonderful Life." 1996.

Wilson, Mrs. Emily D. "I Will Pilot Thee." 1927.

Supporting Material

America West Drilling Company. Pipe Dogs lifting and setting tools. accessed November 8, 2023. https://americawestdrillingsupply.com/pipe-dogs-pipe-lifting-and-setting/.

Bickel, Amy. Kansas-Agland. "'Betrayed by a Fingerprint' Kansas' Fleagle Gang.'" *The Hutchinson News*. (Hutchinson, Kansas). January 28, 2016. accessed November 8, 2023. https://www.hutchnews.com > local "Betrayed by a Fingerprint" Kansas' Fleagle Gang.

Kansas Historical Society. "Jackrabbit Drives." March 2009. accessed November 6, 2023. https://www.kshs.org/kansapedia/jackabbit-drives/12097.

Moxley, Max. "Rice County History…Then and Now." accessed November 6, 2023. https://sterling.digitalsckls.info/history-of-sterling.

National WWII Museum. "'Angels of Okinawa.'": The F4U Corsair. May 3, 2020. accessed November 6, 2023. https://www.nationalww2museum.org "Angels of Okinawa".

Naval History and Heritage Command. "Higgins Boats." July 22, 2021. accessed November 6, 2023. https://www.history.navy.mil Higgins Boats — Naval History and Heritage Command.

Vogt, Martha Nelson, and Christina Vogt. *Searching for Home*. (Hillsboro, Kansas: Triumph Press, 1995).

Voice of America. "American History: US Declares War on Japan, Germany and Italy." accessed November 8, 2023. https://www.51voa.com/VOA_Special_English/American-History-The-United-States-Declares-War-First-on-Japan-Then-Germany-and-Italy--41989.html.

Wikipedia. "Andrew Drumm Institute." October 30, 2023. accessed November 6, 2023. https://en.wikipedia.org/wiki/Andrew_Drumm_Institute.

Wikipedia. "City of St. Louis (train)." September 4, 2023. accessed November 6, 2023. https://en.wikipedia.org/wiki/City_of_St._Louis_(train).

Wikipedia. "JAARS." November 1, 2023. accessed November 6, 2023. https://en.m.wikipedia.org JAARS.

Wikipedia. "Lockheed P-2 Neptune." November 3, 2023. accessed November 6, 2023. https://en.wikipedia.org/wiki/Lockheed_P-2_Neptune.

Wikipedia. "Naval Air Technical Training Center Ward Island." July 14, 2023. accessed November 6, 2023. https://en.wikipedia.org/wiki/Naval_Air_Technical_Training_Center_Ward_Island.

Wilma, David. "Sand Point Naval Air Station: 1920–1970." HistoryLink. org Essay 2249. Accessed November 6, 2023. April 3, 2000. https://www.historylink.org/file/2249. https://www.historylink.org/file/2249.

MILITARY RECORD

DONALD BLAND

High School: 9-43 – 6-46
Education: 11 years
Ancel H. Dugan: Legal Guardian (Assigned)
Place of Enlistment: Kansas City
Skills: Grocery Store, Part-time Clerk, Filling Station Attendant,
    Farm Hand, Small Grain

Rank: AS, USN

Date	Where Stationed
11-26-46	Enlistment
10-26-27	Birthdate on Abstract of Service
11-29-46 – 3-10-47	U.S. Naval Training Center, San Diego 33, CA
3-13-47 – 9-29-47	Naval Air Tech. Training Center, Ward Island, Corpus Christi, Texas
10-3-47 – 10-23-47	USN REC Sta. SD, Nav. S.I.A. (San Diego)

Rank: S1 — Seaman 1st Class

Date	Where Stationed
10-24-47 – 1-19-48	US Naval Training Center San Diego

Rank: SN — Seaman

Date	Where Stationed
4-2-48	Navy Training Center San Diego

Rank: Storekeeper 3rd Class

Date	Where Stationed
4-16-48	U.S. Navy Training Center San Diego
4-7-49	San Diego 33, CA
4-8-48 – 1-9-50	USNAS, San Diego

Rank: AN — Air Navy to AKAN

Date	Where Stationed
1-16-50 – 8-17-50	FAS Ron 112 (Fleet Air Service) Whidbey Island, WN Squadron 112
8-18-50	Transferred to Kodiak, AK
10-25-50	Extension of Enlistment for 1 year
8-23-50 – 2-14-51	FAS Ron 114 Kodiak
3-20-51 – 10-12-51	FAS Ron — NAS Whidbey Island, WN

Rank: AKAN to AK3

Date	Where Stationed
4-16-51	FAS Ron — NAS Whidbey Island, WN
10-12-51 – 10-18-51	FADU (CFS) NAS Whidbey Island, WN
10-25-51	Discharge

Date	Rank	Unit
12-31-50	AN	FAS 114
2-15-51	AKAN	FAS 114
3-31-51	Less than a month	FAS 112
6-30-51	AK3	VP FAS Ron 112
10-15-51	AK3	Transferred VP FAS Ron 112
10-25-51	AK3	FADU ComFair Seattle